Wole Soyinka:

An Appraisal

Edited by Adewale Maja-Pearce

...ublishers
...rs (Oxford) Ltd
...ord OX2 8EJ

Heinemann: A Division of Reed Publishing (USA) Inc.
361 Hanover Street, Portsmouth, NH 03801–3912, USA

Heinemann Educational Books (Nigeria) Ltd
PMB 5205, Ibadan
Heinemann Educational Boleswa
PO Box 10103, Village Post Office, Gaborone, Botswana

FLORENCE   PRAGUE   PARIS   MADRID
ATHENS   MELBOURNE   JOHANNESBURG
AUCKLAND   SINGAPORE   TOKYO
CHICAGO   SAO PAULO

First published by Heinemann Educational Publishers in 1994

British Library Cataloguing in Publication Data
A catalogue record for this book is available from the British Library.

Cover design by Simon Stafford, Stafford and Stafford

ISBN 0435 911511

Phototypeset by
Wilmaset Ltd, Birkenhead, Wirral
Printed and bound in Great Britain
by Clays Ltd, St Ives plc

94 95 96 97 98 10 9 8 7 6 5 4 3 2 1

'For me, justice is the first condition of humanity.'

WOLE SOYINKA: *The Man Died*

Contents

Foreword

An appraisal to mark Wole Soyinka's sixtieth birthday hardly requires any justification. His achievement as one of the most original and multifarious of Africa's writers was recognised long before the award of the Nobel Prize for Literature in 1986, since when his astonishing output – plays, novels, poems, autobiography, essays, social commentary – has continued unabated. Chinua Achebe, himself a contender for the prize, spoke of Soyinka's 'stupendous energy and vitality'[1] at the time of the award; and Femi Osofisan, the most highly regarded of the 'second generation' of Nigerian playwrights, paid him perhaps the ultimate accolade when he subsequently declared that 'the dialogue with Soyinka has hardly begun. He represents strength and versatility in our artistic life and for me I can't but respond to that.'[2]

Needless to say, there is all the difference in the world between the creative response of a fellow writer, of whom Osofisan himself is such an examplar, and the 'wearisome thesists'[3] of an apparently insatiable academic industry, whose agenda seems to have increasingly less to do with the illumination of the work under scrutiny than the advancement of self-justifying careers. Soyinka especially has been ill served by the more extremist tendencies within this industry, as he himself has long recognised:

> My concern is to situate the 'critic' in his sociological actuality, an actuality little known outside a closed 'ivory' circle, an actuality made up of those calculating, trite, opportunistic motivations which lead the critic to abandon – if he ever had one – a genuine concern for the literary corpus or the triggering cultural mechanisms of a society.[4]

It was against this background that the essays collected here were first conceived: to engage with the man and his work at the appropriate level of seriousness commensurate with his achievement. The key, of course, lay in the contributors themselves, some of whom were content to register their regard and leave it at that, others of whom adopted a more critical stance, but only out of 'a genuine concern for the literary corpus', and always with the knowledge of 'the triggering cultural mechanisms' of Soyinka's own society. I might add that the alacrity with which all the contributors responded to my initial request was itself a comment on the esteem in which he is held both within Nigeria and abroad.

I have also taken the opportunity here to reproduce Soyinka's Nobel lecture. The fact that it deals mostly with a South Africa that has undergone profound changes in the intervening years seemed to me less important than the example it offered of Soyinka's abiding concern with injustice. This concern is most forcefully expressed in the lengthy interview with which this collection ends. The interview itself was conducted only days after the military government in Nigeria saw fit to subvert the democratic process following the triumph of the 'wrong' candidate in the elections which the same military government had organised as proof of its apparent commitment to the ideals of the New World Order. Living in the interregnum indeed: as the old dies and the new struggles to be born, the great diversity of morbid symptoms arrayed before us exceed even our most unsettling nightmares; but whatever the immediate outcome of this, by now all too familiar, denigration of the popular will, including the very future of the country as a viable entity, we know at least that the eventual success of democracy will be due in part to those who have consistently refused to remain silent in the face of tyranny. I trust that this offering is fitting tribute.

ADEWALE MAJA-PEARCE, OXFORD, 1994

1 'An event to celebrate', *The African Guardian* (Lagos), 30 October 1986, p. 16.

2 Chris Dunton: 'Theatre as a game' (An interview with Femi Osofisan), *West Africa*, 24–30 April 1989, p. 647.

3 Wole Soyinka: 'Who's Afraid of Elesin Oba?' in *Art, Dialogue and Outrage: Essays on Literature and Culture*, Ibadan: New Horn Press, 1988, p. 112.

4 Wole Soyinka: 'Responses in Kind', in *Art, Dialogue and Outrage*, ibid, p. 269.

Nobel Lecture 1986:
This Past Must Address Its Present

WOLE SOYINKA

Dedicated to Nelson Mandela

A rather curious scene, unscripted, once took place in the wings of a London theatre at the same time as the scheduled performance was being presented on the actual stage, before an audience. What happened was this: an actor refused to come on stage for his allocated role. Action was suspended. A fellow actor tried to persuade him to emerge, but he stubbornly shook his head. Then a struggle ensued. The second actor had hoped that, by suddenly exposing the reluctant actor to the audience in full glare of the spotlight, he would have no choice but to rejoin the cast. And so he tried to take the delinquent actor by surprise, pulling him suddenly towards the stage. He did not fully succeed, so a brief but untidy struggle began. The unwilling actor was completely taken aback and deeply embarrassed – some of that tussle was quite visible to a part of the audience.

The performance itself, it should be explained, was an improvisation around an incident. This meant that the actors were free, within the convention of the performance, to stop, re-work any part they wished, invite members of the audience on stage, assign roles and change costumes in full view of the audience. They therefore could also dramatise their wish to have that unco-operative actor join them – which they did with gusto. That actor had indeed left the stage before the contentious scene began. He had served notice during rehearsals that he would not participate in it. In the end, he had his way but the incident proved very troubling to him for weeks afterwards. He found himself compelled to puzzle out this clash in

1

attitudes between himself and his fellow writers and performers. He experienced, on the one hand, an intense rage that he had been made to appear incapable of confronting a stark reality, made to appear to suffer from interpretative coyness, to seem inhibited by a cruel reality or perhaps to carry his emotional involvement with an event so far as to interfere with his professional will. Of course, he knew that it was none of these things. The truth was far simpler. Unlike his colleagues together with whom he shared, unquestionably, the same political attitude towards the event which was being represented, he found the mode of presentation at war with the ugliness it tried to convey, creating an intense disquiet about his very presence on that stage, in that place, before an audience whom he considered collectively responsible for that dehumanising actuality.

And now let us remove some of the mystery and make that incident a little more concrete. The scene was the Royal Court Theatre, London, 1958. It was one of those Sunday nights which were given to experimentation, an innovation of that remarkable theatre manager-director, George Devine, whose creative nurturing radicalised British theatre of that period and produced later icons like John Osborne, N.F. Simpson, Edward Bond, Arnold Wesker, Harold Pinter, John Arden etc., and even forced the then conservative British palate to sample stylistic and ideological pariahs like Samuel Beckett and Bertolt Brecht. On this particular occasion, the evening was devoted to a form of 'living' theatre, and the main fare was titled *Eleven Men Dead at Hola*. The actors were not all professional actors; indeed they were mostly writers who jointly created and performed these dramatic pieces. Those with a long political memory may recall what took place at Hola Camp, Kenya, during the Mau-Mau Liberation struggle. The British colonial power believed that the Mau-Mau could be smashed by herding Kenyans into special camps, trying to separate the hard cases, the mere suspects and the potential recruits – oh, they had it all neatly worked out. One such camp was Hola Camp and the incident involved the death of eleven of the detainees who were simply beaten to death by camp officers and warders. The usual enquiry was set up, and it was indeed the Report which provided the main text on which the performance was based.

We need now only identify the reluctant actor and, if you have not guessed that by now – it was none other than this speaker. I recall the occasion as vividly as actors are wont to recollect for ever and ever the frightening moment of a blackout, when the lines are not only forgotten but even the moment in the play. The role which I had been assigned was that of a camp guard, one of the killers. We were equipped with huge night-sticks and, while a narrator read the testimony of one of the guards, our task was to raise the cudgels slowly and, almost ritualistically, bring them down on the necks and shoulders of the prisoners, under orders of the white camp officers. A surreal scene. Even in rehearsals, it was clear that the end product would be a surrealist tableau. The Narrator at a lectern under a spot; a dispassionate reading, deliberately clinical, letting the stark facts reveal the states of mind of torturers and victims. A small ring of white officers, armed. One seizes a cudgel from one of the warders to demonstrate how to beat a human being without leaving visible marks. Then the innermost clump of detainees, their only weapon – non-violence. They had taken their decision to go on strike, refused to go to work unless they obtained better camp conditions. So they squatted on the ground and refused to move, locked their hands behind their knees in silent defiance. Orders were given. The inner ring of guards, the blacks, moved in, lifted the bodies by hooking their hands underneath the armpits of the detainees, carried them like toads in a state of petrification to one side, divided them into groups.

The faces of the victims were impassive; they are resolved to offer no resistance. The beatings begin: one to the left side, then the back, the arms – right, left, front, back. Rythmically. The cudgels swing in unison. The faces of the white guards glow with professional satisfaction, their arms gesture languidly from time to time, suggesting it is time to shift to the next batch, or beat a little more severely on the neglected side. In terms of images, a fluid, near balletic scene.

Then the contrast, the earlier official version, enacting how the prisoners were supposed to have died. This claimed that the prisoners had collapsed, that they died after drinking from a poisoned water supply. So we staged that also. The prisoners filed to the water waggon, gasping with thirst. After the first two or three had drunk and commenced writhing with pain, these humane guards rushed to stop the others but no, they were already wild with thirst, fought their way past salvation and drank greedily from the same source. The groans spread from one to the other, the writhing, the collapse – then agonised deaths. That was the version of the camp governors.

The motif was simple enough, the theatrical format a tried and tested one, faithful to a particular convention. What then was the problem? It was one, I believe, that affects most writers. When is play-acting rebuked by reality? When is fictionalising presumptuous? What happens after play-acting? One of the remarkable properties of the particular theatrical convention I have just described is that it gives off a strong odour of perenniality, that feeling of 'I have been here before'. 'I have been witness to this.' 'The past enacts its presence.' In such an instance, that sense of perenniality can serve both as exorcism, a certificate of release or indeed – especially for the audience – a soporific. We must bear in mind that at the time of presentation, and to the major part of that audience, every death of a freedom fighter was a notch on a gun, the death of a fiend, an animal, a bestial mutant, not the martyrdom of a patriot.

We know also, however, that such efforts can provoke changes, that an actualisation of the statistical, journalistic footnote can arouse revulsion in the complacent mind, leading to the beginning of a commitment to change, redress. And on this occasion, angry questions had been raised in the Houses of Parliament. Liberals, humanitarians and reformists had taken up the cause of justice for the victims. Some had even travelled to Kenya to obtain details which exposed the official lie. This profound unease which paralysed my creative will, therefore reached beyond the audience and, finally, I traced its roots to my own feelings of assaulted humanity, and its clamour for a different form of response. It provoked a feeling of indecency about that presentation, rather like the deformed arm of a leper which is thrust at the healthy to provoke a charitable sentiment. This, I believe, was the cause of that intangible, but totally visceral rejection which thwarted the demands of my calling, rendered it inadequate and mocked the empathy of my colleagues. It was as if the inhuman totality, of which that scene was a mere fragment, was saying to us: Kindly keep your comfortable sentiment to yourselves.

Of course, I utilise that episode only as illustration of the far deeper internalised processes of the creative mind, a process that endangers the writer in two ways: he either freezes up completely or, he abandons the pen for far more direct means of contesting unacceptable reality. And again, Hola Camp provides a convenient means of approaching that aspect of my continent's reality which, for us whom it directly affronts, constitutes the greatest threat to global peace in our actual existence. For there is a gruesome appropriateness in the fact that an African, a black man, should stand here today, in the same year that the progressive prime minister of this host country was murdered, in the same year as Samora Machel was brought down on the territory of the desperate last-ditch guardians of the theory of racial superiority which has brought so much misery to our common humanity. Whatever the facts are about Olof Palme's death, there can be no question about his life. To the racial oppression of a large sector of humanity, Olof Palme pronounced, and acted, a decisive No! Perhaps it was those who were outraged by this act of racial 'treachery' who were myopic enough to imagine that the death of an individual would arrest the march of his convictions; perhaps it was simply yet another instance of the Terror Epidemic that feeds today on shock, not reason. It does not matter; an authentic conscience of the white tribe has been stilled, and the loss is both yours and mine. Samora Machel, the leader who once placed his country on a war footing against South Africa, went down in as yet mysterious circumstances. True, we are all still haunted by the Nkomati Accord which negated that earlier triumphant moment of the African collective will; nevertheless, his foes across the border have good reason to rejoice over his demise and, in that sense, his death is, ironically, a form of triumph for the black race.

Is that perhaps too stark a paradox? Then let me take you back to Hola Camp. It is cattle which are objects of the stick, or whip. So are horses, goats, donkeys etc. Their definition therefore involves being occasionally beaten to death. If, thirty years after Hola Camp, it is at all thinkable that it takes the ingenuity of the most sophisticated electronic interference to kill an African resistance

fighter, the champions of racism are already admitting to themselves what they continue to deny to the world: that they, white
supremacist breed, have indeed come a long way in their definition
of their chosen enemy since Hola Camp. They have come an
incredibly long way since Sharpeville when they shot unarmed,
fleeing Africans in the back. They have come very far since 1930
when, at the first organised incident of the burning of passes, the
South African blacks decided to turn Dingaan's Day, named for the
defeat of the Zulu leader Dingaan, into a symbol of affirmative
resistance by publicly destroying their obnoxious passes. In response to those thousands of passes burnt on Cartright Flats, the
Durban police descended on the unarmed protesters killing some
half dozen and wounding hundreds. They backed it up with a
scorched earth campaign which dispersed thousands of Africans
from their normal environment, victims of imprisonment and
deportation. And even that 1930 repression was a quantum leap
from that earlier, spontaneous protest against the Native Pass law
in 1919, when the police merely rode down the protesters on
horseback, whipped and sjamboked them, chased and harried
them, like stray goats and wayward cattle, from street corner to
shanty lodge. Every act of racial terror, with its vastly increasing
sophistication of style and escalation in human loss, is itself an
acknowledgement of improved knowledge and respect for the
potential of what is feared, an acknowledgement of the sharpening
tempo of triumph by the victimised.

   For there was this aspect which struck me most forcibly in that
attempt to recreate the crime at Hola Camp: in the various
testimonies of the white officers, it stuck out, whether overtly
stated or simply through their efficient detachment from the
ongoing massacre. It was this: at no time did these white overseers
actually experience the human 'otherness' of their victims. They
clearly did not experience the reality of the victims as human
beings. Animals perhaps, a noxious form of vegetable life maybe,
but certainly not human. I do not speak here of their colonial
overlords, the ones who formulated and sustained the policy of
settler colonialism, the ones who dispatched the Maxim guns and
tuned the imperial bugle. They knew very well that empires existed
which had to be broken, that civilisations had endured for centuries

which had to be destroyed. The 'sub-human' denigration for which their 'civilising mission' became the altruistic remedy, was the mere rationalising icing on the cake of imperial greed. But yes indeed, there were the agents, those who carried out orders (like Eichmann, to draw parallels from the white continent); they – whether as bureaucrats, technicians or camp governors – had no conceptual space in their heads which could be filled – except very rarely and exceptionally – by 'the black as *also* human'. It would be correct to say that this has remained the pathology of the average South African white since the turn of the last century to this moment. Here, for example, is one frank admission by an enlightened, even radical mind of that country:

It was not until my last year in school that it had occurred to me that these black people, these voteless masses, were in any way concerned with the socialism which I professed or that they had any role to play in the great social revolution which in these days seemed to be imminent. The 'workers' who were destined to inherit the new world were naturally the white carpenters and bricklayers, the tramworkers and miners who were organised in their trade unions and who voted for the Labour Party. I would no more have thought of discussing politics with a native youth than of inviting him home to play with me or to a meal or asking him to join the Carnarvon Football Club. The African was on a different plane, hardly human, part of the scene as were dogs and trees and, more remotely, cows. I had no special feelings about him, not interest nor hate nor love. He just did not come into my social picture. So completely had I accepted the traditional attitudes of the time.

Yes, I believe that this self-analysis by Eddie Roux, the Afrikaner political rebel and scientist, remains today the flat, unvarnished truth for the majority of Afrikaners. 'No special feelings . . . not interest nor hate nor love', the result of a complete acceptance of 'traditional attitudes'. That passage captures a mind's racial *tabula rasa*, if you like, in the first decade of this century – about the time, in short, when the Nobel series of prizes was inaugurated. But a slate, no matter how clean, cannot avoid receiving impressions once it is exposed to air – fresh or polluted. And we are now in the year 1986, that is after an entire century of direct, intimate exposure, since that confrontation, that first rejection of the dehumanising label implicit in the Native Pass Laws.

Eddie Roux, like hundreds, even thousands of his countrymen, soon made rapid strides. His race has produced its list of martyrs in the cause of non-racialism – one remembers, still with a tinge of pain, Ruth First, destroyed by a letter bomb delivered by the long arm of Apartheid. There are others – André Brink, Abram Fischer, Helen Suzman, Breyten Breytenbach – with the scars of martyrdom still seared into their souls. Intellectuals, writers, scientists, plain working men, politicians – they come to that point where a social reality can no longer be observed as a culture on a slide beneath the microscope, nor turned into aesthetic variations on pages, canvas or the stage. The blacks of course are locked into an unambiguous condition: on this occasion I do not need to address *us*. We know, and we embrace our mission. It is the *other* that this precedent seizes the opportunity to address, and not merely those who are trapped within the confines of that doomed camp, but those who live outside, on the fringes of conscience. Those specifically, who with shameless smugness invent arcane moral propositions that enable them to plead inaction in a language of unparalleled political flatulence; 'Personally, I find sanctions morally repugnant.' Or what shall we say of another leader for whom economic sanctions which work against an eastern European country will not work in the Apartheid enclave of South Africa, that master of histrionics who takes to the world's airwaves to sing, 'Let Poland be' but turns off his hearing aid when the world shouts: 'Let Nicaragua be'. But enough of these world leaders of double-talk and multiple moralities.

It is baffling to any mind that pretends to the slightest claim to rationality, it is truly and formidably baffling. Can the same terrain of phenomenal assimilation – that is, one which produced evidence of a capacity to translate empirical observations into implications of rational human conduct – can this same terrain which, over half a century ago, fifty entire years, two, three generations ago produced the Buntings, the Roux, the Douglas Woltons, Solly Sachs, the Gideon Bothas – can that same terrain, fifty, sixty, even seventy years later, be peopled by a species of humanity so ahistorical that the declaration, so clearly spelt out in 1919 at the burning of the passes, remains only a troublesome event of no enduring significance?

Some atavistic bug is at work here which defies all scientific explanation, an arrest in time within the evolutionary mandate of nature, which puts all human experience of learning to serious question! We have to ask ourselves then, what event can speak to such a breed of people? How do we reactivate that petrified cell which houses historic apprehension and development? Is it possible perhaps that events, gatherings such as this, might help? Dare we skirt the edge of hubris and say to them: Take a good look. Provide your response. In your anxiety to prove that this moment is not possible, you have killed, maimed, silenced, tortured, exiled, debased and dehumanised hundreds of thousands encased in this very skin, crowned with such hair, proudly content with their very being? How many potential partners in the science of heart transplants have you wasted? How do we know how many black South African scientists and writers would have stood here, by now, if you had had the vision to educate the rest of the world in the value of a great multi-racial society?

Jack Cope surely sums it up in his Foreword to *The Adversary Within*, a study of dissidence in Afrikaner literature, when he states:

> Looking back from the perspective of the present, I think it can justly be said that, at the core of the matter, the Afrikaner leaders in 1924 took the wrong turning. Themselves the victims of imperialism in its most evil aspect, all their sufferings and enormous loss of life nevertheless failed to convey to them the obvious historical lesson. They became themselves the new imperialists. They took over from Britain the mantle of empire and colonialism. They could well have set their faces against annexation, aggression, colonial exploitation and oppression, racial arrogance and barefaced hypocrisy, of which they had been themselves the victims. They could have opened the doors to humane ideas and civilizing processes and transformed the great territory with its incalculable resources into another New World.

Instead they deliberately set the clock back wherever they could. Taking over ten million indigenous subjects from British colonial rule, they stripped them of what limited rights they had gained over a century and tightened the screws on their subjection.

Well, perhaps the wars against Shaka and Dingaan and Dingiswayo, even the Great Trek were then too fresh in your *laager* memory. But we are saying that over a century has passed since then, a century in which the world has leapt, in comparative tempo with the past, at least three centuries. And we have seen the potential of man and woman – of all races – contend with the most jealously guarded sovereignty of Nature and the Cosmos. In every field, both in the Humanities and Sciences, we have seen that human creativity has confronted and tempered the hostility of his environment, adapting, moderating, converting, harmonising and even subjugating. Triumphing over errors and resuming the surrendered fields, when man has had time to lick his wounds and listen again to the urgings of his spirit. History – distorted, opportunistic renderings of history have been cleansed and restored to truthful reality, because the traducers of the history of others have discovered that the further they advanced, the more their very progress was checked and vitiated by the lacunae they had purposefully inserted in the history of others. Self-interest dictated yet another round of revisionism – slight, niggardly concessions to begin with. But a breach had been made in the dam and an avalanche proved the logical progression. From the heart of jungles, even before the aid of high-precision cameras mounted on orbiting satellites, civilisations have resurrected, documenting their own existence with unassailable iconography and art. More amazing still, the records of the ancient voyagers, the merchant adventurers of the age when Europe did not yet require to dominate territories in order to feed its industrial mills – those objective recitals of mariners and adventurers from antiquity confirmed what the archaeological remains affirmed so loudly. They spoke of living communities which regulated their own lives, which had evolved a working relationship with Nature, which ministered to their own wants and secured their future with their own genius. These narratives, uncluttered by the impure motives which needed to mystify the plain self-serving rush to dismantle independent societies for easy plundering – pointed accusing fingers unerringly in the direction of European savants, philosophers, scientists and theorists of human evolution. Gobineau is a notorious name, but how many students of European thought today, even among us Africans, recall that several of the most revered names in European philosophy – Hegel, Locke, Montesquieu, Hume, Voltaire – an endless list – were unabashed theorists of racial superiority and denigrators of the African history and being? As for the more prominent names among the theorists of revolution and class struggle – we will draw the curtain of extenuation on their own intellectual aberration, forgiving them a little for their vision of an end to human exploitation.

In any case, the purpose is not really to indict the past, but to summon it to the attention of a suicidal, anachronistic present. To say to that mutant present: you are a child of those centuries of lies, distortion and opportunism in high places, even among the holy of holies of intellectual objectivity. But the world is growing up, while you wilfully remain a child, a stubborn, self-destructive child, with certain destructive powers, but a child nevertheless. And to say to the world, to call attention to its own historic passage of lies – as yet unabandoned by some – which sustains the evil precosity of this child. Wherein then lies the surprise that we, the victims of that intellectual dishonesty of others, demand from that world that is finally coming to itself, a measure of expiation? Demand that it rescue itself, by concrete acts, from the stigma of being the wilful parent of a monstrosity, especially as that monstrous child still draws material nourishment, breath and human recognition from the strengths and devises of that world, with an umbilical cord which stretches across oceans, even across the cosmos via so-called programmes of technological co-operation. We are saying very simply but urgently: Sever that cord. By any name, be it Total Sanction, Boycott, Disinvestment or whatever, sever this umbilical cord and leave this monster of a birth to atrophy and die or to rebuild itself on long-denied humane foundations. Let it collapse, shorn of its external sustenance, let it collapse of its own social disequilibrium, its economic lopsidedness, its war of attrition on its most productive labour. Let it wither like an aborted foetus of the human family if it persists in smothering the minds and sinews which constitute its authentic being.

This pariah society that is Apartheid South Africa plays many games on human intelligence. Listen to this for example. When the whole world escalated its appeal for the release of Nelson Mandela, the South African Government blandly declared that it continued to hold Nelson Mandela for the same reasons that the Allied powers continued to hold Rudolf Hess! Now a statement like that is an obvious appeal to the love of the ridiculous in everyone. Certainly it wrung a kind of satiric poem out of me – Rudolf Hess as Nelson Mandela in blackface! What else can a writer do to protect his humanity against such egregious assaults! But yet again to equate Nelson Mandela to the arch-criminal Rudolf Hess is a macabre improvement on the attitude of regarding him as sub-human. It belongs on that same scale of Apartheid's self-improvement as the ratio between Sharpeville and Von Brandis Square, that near-kind, near-considerate, almost benevolent dispersal of the first Native Pass rebellion.

That world which is so conveniently traduced by Apartheid thought is of course that which I so wholeheartedly embrace, and this is my choice – among several options – of the significance of my presence here. It is a world that nourishes my being, one which is so self-sufficient, so replete in all aspects of its productivity, so confident in itself and in its destiny that it experiences no fear in reaching out to others and in responding to the reach of others. It is the heartstone of our creative existence. It constitutes the prism of our world perception and this means that our sight need not be and has never been permanently turned inwards. If it were, we could not so easily understand the enemy on our doorstep, nor under-stand how to obtain the means to disarm it. When this society which is Apartheid South Africa indulges from time to time in appeals to the outside world that it represents the last bastion of civilisation against the hordes of barbarism from its North, we can even afford an indulgent smile. It is sufficient, imagines this state, to raise the spectre of a few renegade African leaders, psychopaths and robber barons who we ourselves are victims of – whom we denounce before the world and overthrow when we are able – this Apartheid society insists to the world that its picture of the future is the reality which only its policies can erase. This is a continent which only destroys, it proclaims, it is peopled by a race which has never contributed anything positive to the world's pool of knowledge. A vacuum, that will suck into its insatiable maw the entire fruits of centuries of European civilisation, then spew out the resulting mush with contempt. How strange that a society which claims to represent this endangered face of progress should itself be locked in centuries-old fantasies, blithely unaware of, or indifferent to, the fact that it is the last, institutionally functioning product of archaic articles of faith in Euro-Judaic thought.

Take God and Law for example, especially the former. The black race has more than sufficient historic justification to be a little paranoid about the intrusion of alien deities into its destiny. For even today, Apartheid's mentality of the pre-ordained rests – according to its own unabashed claims – on what I can only describe as incidents in a testamentary Godism – I dare not call it Christianity. The sons of Ham on the one hand; the descendants of Shem on the other. The once pronounced, utterly immutable curse. As for Law, these supremacists base their refusal to concede the right of equal political participation to blacks on a claim that Africans have neither respect for, nor the slightest proclivity for Law – that is, for any arbitrating concept between the individual and the collective.

Even the mildest, liberal, somewhat regretful but contented apologists for Apartheid, for at least some form of Apartheid which is not Apartheid but ensures the *status quo* – even this ambivalent breed bases its case on this lack of the idea of Law in the black mind. I need only refer to a recent contribution to this literature in the form of an autobiography by a famous heart transplant surgeon, one who in his own scientific right has probably been a candidate for a Nobel Prize in the Sciences. Despite constant intellectual encounters on diverse levels, the sad phenomenon persists of Afrikaner minds which, in the words of Eddie Roux, is a product of that complete acceptance of the 'traditional attitudes of the time'.

They have, as already acknowledged, quite 'respectable' intellectual ancestors. Wilhelm Friedrich Hegel, to cite just my favourite example, found it convenient to pretend that the African had not yet developed to the level where he

> . . . attained that realization of any substantial objective existence – as for example, God, or Law – in which the interest of man's volition is involved and in which he realizes his own being.

He continues:

> This distinction between himself as an individual and the univer-sality of his essential being, the African in the uniform, undeve-loped oneness of his existence has not yet attained: so that the knowledge of absolute Being, an Other and a Higher than his individual self, is entirely wanting.

Futile to waste a moment refuting the banal untruthfulness of this claim, I content myself with extracting from it only a lesson which escapes, even today, those who insist that the pinnacle of man's intellectual thrust is the capacity to project his universality in the direction of a Super-Other. There is, I believe, a very healthy school of thought which not only opposes this materially, but has produced effectively structured societies which operate indepen-dently of this seductive, even productively inspiring but extrava-gant fable.

Once we thus overcome the temptation to contest the denial of this feat of imaginative projection to the African, we find ourselves left only with the dispassionate exercise of examining in what areas we encounter differences between the histories of societies which, according to Hegel and company, never conceived of this Omnipo-tent Extrusion into Infinite Space, and those who did – be these differences in the areas of economic or artistic life, social relations or scientific attainment – in short, in all those activities which are empirically verifiable, quite different from the racial consequences of imprecations arising from that post Adam-and-Eve nudist escapade in the Old Testament.

When we do this, we come upon a curious fact. The pre-colonial history of African societies – and I refer to both Euro-Christian and Arab-Islamic colonisation – indicates very clearly that African societies never at any time of their existence went to war with another over the issue of *their* religion. That is, at no time did the black race attempt to subjugate or forcibly convert others with any holier-than-thou evangelising zeal. Economic and political motives, yes. But not religion. Perhaps this unnatural fact was responsible for the conclusions of Hegel – we do not know. Certainly the bloody histories of the world's major religions, localised skirmishes of which extend even to the present, lead to a sneaking suspicion that religion, as defined by these eminent philosophers, comes to self-knowledge only through the activity of war.

When, therefore, towards the close of the twentieth century, that is, centuries after the Crusades and Jihads that laid waste other and one another's civilisations, fragmented ancient cohesive social relations and trampled upon the spirituality of entire peoples, smashing their cultures in obedience to the strictures of unseen gods, when today, we encounter nations whose social reasoning is guided by canonical, theological claims, we believe, on our part, that the era of darkness has never truly left the world. A state whose justification for the continuing suppression of its indigenes, indigenes who constitute the majority on that land, rests on claims to divine selection is a menace to secure global relationships in a world that thrives on nationalism as common denominator. Such a society does not, in other words, belong in this modern world. We also have our myths, but we have never employed them as a base for the subjugation of others. We also inhabit a realistic world, however, and, for the recovery of the fullness of that world, the black race has no choice but to prepare itself and volunteer the supreme sacrifice.

In speaking of that world – both myth and reality – it is our duty, perhaps our very last peaceful duty to a doomed enemy, to remind it, and its supporters outside its boundaries, that the phenomenon of ambivalence induced by the African world has a very long history, but that most proponents of the slanderous aspects have long ago learnt to abandon the untenable. Indeed it is probably even more pertinent to remind this racist society that our African world, its cultural hoards and philosophical thought have had concrete impacts on the racists' own forebears, have proved seminal to a number of movements and even created tributaries, both pure and polluted, among the white indigenes in their own homelands.

Such a variety of encounters and responses have been due, naturally, to profound searches for new directions in their cultural adventures, seeking solaces to counter the remorseless mechanisation of their existence, indeed seeking new meanings for the mystery of life and attempting to overcome the social malaise created by the very triumphs of their own civilisation. It has led to a profound respect for the African contribution to world knowledge, which did not however end the habitual denigration of the African world. It has created in places a near-deification of the African person – that phase in which every African had to be a prince – which, yet again, was coupled with a primitive fear and loathing for the person of the African. To these paradoxical responses, the essentiality of our black being remains untouched. For the black race knows, and is content simply to know, itself. It is the European world that has sought, with the utmost zeal, to re-define itself through these encounters, even when it does appear that he is endeavouring to grant meaning to an experience of the African world.

We can make use of the example of that period of European Expressionism, a movement which saw African art, music and dramatic rituals share the same sphere of influence as the most disparate, astonishingly incompatible collection of ideas, ideologies and social tendencies – Freud, Karl Marx, Bakunin, Nietzsche, cocaine and free love. What wonder then, that the spiritual and plastic presences of the Bakota, Nimba, the Yoruba, Dogon, Dan etc. should find themselves at once the inspiration and the anathematised of a delirium that was most peculiarly European, mostly Teutonic and Gallic, spanning at least four decades across the last and the present centuries. Yet the vibrant goal remained the complete liberation of man, that freeing of his yet untapped potential that would carve marble blocks for the constructing of a new world, debourgeoisify existing constrictions of European thought and light the flame to forge a new fraternity throughout this brave new world. Yes, within this single movement that covered the vast spectrum of outright fascism, anarchism and revolutionary communism, the reality that was Africa was, as always, sniffed at, delicately tested, swallowed entire, regurgitated, appropriated, extolled and damned in the revelatory frenzy of a continent's recreative energies.

Oskar Kokoschka for instance: for this dramatist and painter African ritualism led mainly in the direction of sadism, sexual perversion, general self-gratification. It flowed naturally into a Nietzschean apocalyptic summons, full of self-induced, ecstatic rage against society, indeed, against the world. Vassily Kandinsky, on his part, responded to the principles of African art by foreseeing:

> . . . a science of art erected on a broad foundation which must be international in character.

insisting that

> It is interesting, but certainly not sufficient, to create an exclusively European art theory.

The science of art would then lead, according to him, to

> a comprehensive synthesis which will extend far beyond the confines of art into the realm of the oneness of the human and the 'divine'.

This same movement, whose centenary will be due for celebrations in European artistic capitals in the next decade or two – among several paradoxes the phenomenon of European artists of later acknowledged giant stature – Modigliani, Matisse, Gauguin, Picasso, Brancusi etc. worshipping with varying degrees of fervour, at the shrine of African and Polynesian artistic revelations, even as Johannes Becher, in his Expressionist delirium, swore to build a new world on the eradication of all plagues, including –

> Negro tribes, fever, tuberculosis, venereal epidemics, intellectual psychic defects – I'll fight them, vanquish them.

And was it by coincidence that contemporaneously with this stirring manifesto, yet another German enthusiast, Leo Frobenius – with no claims whatever to being part of, or indeed having the least interest in the Expressionist movement – was able to visit Ile-Ife, the heartland and cradle of the Yoruba race, and be profoundly stirred by an object of beauty, the product of the Yoruba mind and hand, a classic expression of that serene portion of the world resolution of that race. In his own words:

> Before us stood a head of marvellous beauty, wonderfully cast in antique bronze, true to the life, encrusted with a patina of glorious dark green. This was, in very deed, the Olokun, Atlantic Africa's Poseidon.

Yet listen to what he had to write about the very people whose handiwork had lifted him into these realms of universal sublimity:

> Profoundly stirred, I stood for many minutes before the remnant of the erstwhile Lord and Ruler of the Empire of Atlantis. My companions were no less astounded. As though we had agreed to do so, we held our peace. Then I looked around and saw – the blacks – the circle of the sons of the 'venerable priest', his Holiness the Oni's friends, and his intelligent officials. I was moved to silent melancholy at the thought that this assembly of degenerate and feeble-minded posterity should be the legitimate guardians of so much loveliness.

A direct invitation to a free-for-all race for dispossession, justified on the grounds of the keeper's unworthiness, it recalls other schizophrenic conditions which are mother to, for instance, the far more lethal, dark mythopoeia of Van Wyk Louw. For though this erstwhile Nazi sympathiser would later rain maledictions on the heads of the more extreme racists of his countrymen –

> Lord, teach us to think what 'own' is, Lord let us think! and then: over hate against blacks, browns, whites: over this and its cause I dare to call down judgement.

– Van Wyk's powerful epic *Raka* was guaranteed to churn up the white cesspools of these primordial fears. A work of searing, visceral impact operating on racial memory, it would feed the

Afrikaner Credo on the looming spectre of a universal barbaric recession, bearing southwards on the cloven hooves of the Fifth Horseman of the Apocalypse, the black.

There is a deep lesson for the world in the black races' capacity to forgive, one which, I often think, has much to do with ethical precepts which spring from their world view and authentic religions, none of which is ever totally eradicated by the accretions of foreign faiths and their implicit ethnocentricisms. For, not content with being a racial slanderer, one who did not hesitate to denigrate, in such uncompromisingly nihilistic terms, the ancestral fount of the black races – a belief which this ethnologist himself observed – Frobenius was also a notorious plunderer, one of a long line of European archaeological raiders. The museums of Europe testify to this insatiable lust of Europe; the frustrations of the Ministries of Culture of the Third World and of organisations like UNESCO are a continuing testimony to the tenacity, even recidivist nature of your routine receiver of stolen goods. Yet, is it not amazing that Frobenius is today still honoured by black institutions, black leaders and scholars? That his anniversaries provide ready excuse for intellectual gatherings and symposia on the black continent, that his racist condescensions, assaults have not been permitted to obscure his contribution to the knowledge of Africa, or the role which he has played in the understanding of the phenomenon of human culture and society, even in spite of the frequent patchiness of his scholarship?

It is the same largeness of spirit which has informed the relationship today of erstwhile colonial nations, some of whom have undergone the most cruel forms of settler or plantation colonialism, where the human degradation that goes with greed and exploitation attained such levels of perversion that human ears, hands and noses served to atone for failures in production quota. Nations which underwent the agony of wars of liberation, whose earth freshly teems with the bodies of innocent victims and unsung martyrs, live side by side today with their recent enslavers, even sharing the control of their destiny with those who, barely four or five years ago, compelled them to witness the massacre of their kith and kin. Over and above Christian charity, they are content to rebuild, and share. This spirit of collaboration is easy to dismiss as

the treacherous ploy of that special breed of leaders who settle for
early compromises in order to safeguard, for their own use, the
polished shoes of the departing oppressors. In many cases, the truth
of this must be conceded. But we also have examples of regimes,
allied to the aspirations of their masses on the black continent,
which have adopted this same political philosophy. And, in any
case, the final arbiters are the people themselves, from whose
relationships any observations such as this obtain any validity. Let
us simply content ourselves with remarking that it is a phenomenon
worthy of note. There are, after all, European nations today whose
memory of domination by other races remains so vivid more than
two centuries after liberation, that a terrible vengeance culturally,
socially and politically is still exacted, even at this very moment,
from the descendants of those erstwhile conquerors. I have visited
such nations whose cruel histories under foreign domination are
enshrined as icons to daily consciousness in monuments, parks, in
museums and churches, in documentation, woodcuts and photo-
gravures displayed under bullet-proof glass cases but, most telling
of all, in the reduction of the remnants of the conquering hordes to
the degraded status of aliens on sufferance, with reduced civic
rights, privileges and social status, a barely tolerated marginality
that expresses itself in the pathos of downcast faces, dropped
shoulders and apologetic encounters in those rare times when
intercourse with the latterly assertive race is unavoidable. Yes, all
this I have seen, and much of it has been written about and debated
in international gatherings. And even while acknowledging the
poetic justice of it in the abstract, one cannot help but wonder if a
physical pound of flesh, excised at birth, is not a kinder act than a
lifelong visitation of the sins of the father on the sons even to the
tenth and twelfth generations.

Confronted with such traditions of attenuating the racial and
cultural pride of these marginalised or minority peoples, the mind
travels back to our own societies where such causative histories are
far fresher in the memory, where the ruins of formerly thriving
communities still speak eloquent accusations and the fumes still rise
from the scorched earth strategies of colonial and racist myopia.
Yet the streets bear the names of former oppressors, their statues
and other symbols of subjugation are left to decorate their squares,

the consciousness of a fully confident people having relegated them to mere decorations and roosting-places for bats and pigeons. And the libraries remain unpurged, so that new generations freely browse through the works of Frobenius, of Hume, Hegel or Montesquieu and others without first encountering, freshly stamped on the fly-leaf: WARNING! THIS WORK IS DANGEROUS FOR YOUR RACIAL SELF-ESTEEM.

Yet these proofs of accommodation, on the grand or minuscule scale, collective, institutional or individual, must not be taken as proof of an infinite, uncritical capacity of black patience. They constitute in their own nature, a body of tests, an accumulation of debt, an implicit offer that must be matched by concrete returns. They are the blocks in a suspended bridge begun from one end of a chasm which, whether the builders will it or not, must obey the law of matter and crash down beyond a certain point, settling definitively into the widening chasm of suspicion, frustration, and redoubled hate. On that testing ground which, for us, is Southern Africa, that medieval camp of biblical terrors, primitive suspicions, a choice must be made by all lovers of peace: either to bring it into the modern world, into a rational state of being within that spirit of human partnership, a capacity for which has been so amply demonstrated by every liberated black nation on our continent, or – to bring it abjectly to its knees by ejecting it, in every aspect, from humane recognition, so that it caves in internally, through the strategies of its embattled majority. Whatever the choice, this inhuman affront cannot be allowed to pursue our twentieth-century conscience into the twenty-first, that symbolic coming-of-age which peoples of all cultures appear to celebrate with rites of passage. That calendar, we know, is not universal, but time is, and so are the imperatives of time. And of those imperatives that challenge our being, our presence and humane definition at this time, none can be considered more pervasive than the end of racism, the eradication of human inequality and the dismantling of all their structures. The Prize is the consequent enthronement of its complement: universal suffrage, and peace.

The Complexity of Freedom

WILSON HARRIS

It is my intention to look closely at Wole Soyinka's play *The Road*[1] in this article but before doing so I find it necessary to sketch in rather loosely perhaps but pointedly nevertheless, I hope, certain premises that may help to illumine the significance of the play for me within the paradoxes of this late twentieth-century age.

The complex forces that need to be explored by the critical imagination tend to be swept aside I find at this time and to give way to facile judgements that are in accord with the instant world of the mass media. As a consequence patterns of uniform taste and uniform expectation, uniform sex, uniform violence, bulk large and acquire an involuntary authoritarian texture in the way they govern the consumption of the arts.

This is an uncanny irony. Is it possible that the best-seller obsession in consumer societies hand in hand with the inflation that threatens minority arts may so determine and deaden taste that it becomes an unwitting authoritarian parallel to political monoliths in other so-called socialist areas of the globe?

It is against such questions and such a background that we need, I feel, to address ourselves to the complex forces of freedom in the march of events.

All this could take us far afield but I shall resist the temptation and seize upon but a few illustrations to provide a signal for a certain crisis in tradition that is inherent in the premises I hope to sketch into play quickly as a prelude to an analysis of *The Road*.

Every renaissance is in some degree a crisis of tradition, a crisis of *seeing* or of responding to heterogeneous perspectives that lie half-buried, half-exposed, within the biased conditions of an age that may subconsciously – if not consciously – thwart the prospect of a 're-birth' or a 'resurrection'.

When one uses the term 'renaissance' one thinks automatically of ancient Greece, Rome, and their renewed impact on Europe centuries ago. What is now at stake perhaps is a phenomenon of pre-Columbian American arts and ancient African masks that speak across history and landscapes to Europe and Asia and bear upon every field of imagination.

Individual imaginations tumble into mind whose work sustains some trace or other of this profound encounter. May I pull three names from a mental hat, Pablo Picasso, Henry Moore, Joseph Conrad, and say something briefly about these in the context of paradoxical premises of which I spoke a short while ago as holding out some measure of assistance in our approaches to a world climate of over-shadowed sensibility that relates to Soyinka's achievement in *The Road*.

The originality of Picasso, it seems to me, was stimulated at an early stage by his profound instinct for the 'mathematics' of the African mask and this led him to question symmetries of complacency in Europe and to relate the savage past to the equally savage present in global consciousness.

His Guernica painting with its rhythm of terror and potent insight into embattled freedom was a spectral watershed of surreal art between the two World Wars. With great fame in the middle twentieth century came a slackening of his powers, a glibness, a superficiality, a cynical tendency, it seems to me, to play with consumer expectations and to dash off cartoon-like sketches that sold like hot cakes straight from the oven of genius.

The epic nerve of Henry Moore was nourished at the outset, I believe, by his close dialogue with pre-Columbian American sculptures and artefacts of nature created by wind or rain or fire into metaphors of royal and elemental sensibility.

The pathology or strain – however elegantly concealed – that comes into some of his later figures may reflect, in some degree, the distance that lies between his epic vision of enduring mind and what obtains in a market place of culture ruled by fashion, a distance he may have sought to placate.

Beyond a shadow of doubt Picasso and Moore, different as they are from each other, were nourished by their dialogue with stranger cultures to create shapes that stand upon a frontier which alerts us to a crisis of tradition, a crisis of fate and freedom, a capacity for genuine encounter and dialogue between cultures in dangerous times, on one hand, and on the other frustration or cynicism or elegant pathology born of the need to conspire with deadened appetite or fashionable prejudice within a complacent technology.

And this brings me to literature and to Conrad's involvement with Africa and with Europe, with heterogeneity and with homogeneity.

There is a decisive faculty or break with uniform prejudice in Conrad's *Heart of Darkness* but it is shrouded by the conditions of his age and by the tool of narrative he had inherited from the English homogeneous novel of the eighteenth and nineteenth centuries.

All this is pertinent I think to the intuitive shape that lies in his work and to the frustrations that exist there, the fear of blackness, the *nigredo* (if I may use an alchemical term). There is no decision or originality of gesture and freedom of movement that can be authentic unless as it arises to consciousness it confesses to how it is still masked, in some degree, by the very conditions from which it arises, by past education or propaganda, past or present securities and anxieties, by the historical restriction it partially breaks. And as it so confesses it points intuitively to the reality of freedom, the complexity of freedom, as an unfathomable decision that varies with the cloak of age or biased history it unravels.

Conrad's achievement, it seems to me, in *Heart of Darkness* was to arrive upon a frontier of imagination which his doomed characters, obsessed with *nigredo* or blackness, never crossed. A frontier nevertheless that was an extraordinary achievement at the beginning of the twentieth century. It fused conquest exercised in the name of virtue into moral self-deception. We see it on another level, I would suggest, in the manual of seamanship that Marlow prizes which symbolises order on a technological plane only to enhance all the more darkly Kurtz's manifesto of light and goodness that are extolled above a postscript or confession 'Exterminate all the brutes'.

Does order breed extermination of others in the name of purity or virtue?

The twentieth century is all too familiar with such grim ideology.

By and large Conrad's 'eclipse of the word' is an intuitive parable woven into the fiction he wrote to indicate that a narrative tool governed by absolute ruling image to sustain meaning may indeed apparently simplify a structure of meaning by voiding all other difficult perspectives but its clarity so-called is an eclipse at the same time, it is an illusion.

The implications are strange but true, I believe. A narrative tool or habit of command that exercises itself as perfectly natural, perfectly beautiful and normal within a *homogeneous* cultural imperative, where it is rooted in consenting classes and common values, builds into itself an equation of inner eclipse as it generates the suppression of others in a *heterogeneous* situation. That was the frontier of paradox between Europe and Africa that *Heart of Darkness* achieved. Conrad went no further. His despair becomes more and more marked and inner eclipse stops short of inner space or transformed narrative tool and medium of consciousness.

Indeed any advance beyond that frontier on which *Heart of Darkness* stands continues to arouse – three-quarters of a century later – identical realistic (so-called) prejudices and misgivings in a world that remains consistently in pawn to vested interests, to ideologies of conquest in politics, industry, statecraft, and to the polarisation of cultures.

In this bleak context, it would seem to me, what is required at a certain level – if a new dialogue is to begin to emerge – is a penetration of partial images, *not* a submission to the traditional reinforcement of partiality into total or absolute institution; partiality may then begin to declare itself for what it is and to acquire a re-creative susceptibility to otherness in a new and varied evolution of community within a fabric of images in fiction and drama; it may begin to evoke inner links or correspondences with stranger cultures (that in their turn confess to their recreative partiality and new susceptibility), so that all in all a movement occurs towards a goal of profound self-awareness, a goal that remains ceaselessly unfinished or drawn towards futurity in an intricate play of partial image upon partial image open to mutual re-visualisations, intricate exploration backwards and forwards within a world that alters to re-educate itself into flexible limits in the living we take for granted as exploiters and exploited, in the dead whose tongues of fire we need to cultivate into reflexes of self-judgement.

It is within such premises and in the light of such challenges that I would now like to turn to Soyinka's play *The Road*.

In the note *For The Producer* which follows *Characters* we are told of a 'transition from the human to the divine essence' and this begins to prepare us for a Quest which is 'part psychic, part intellectual grope'. The paradox at the heart of that grope is 'the dance' which is both 'the movement of transition' and 'visual suspension of death'.

All this may seem difficult but it becomes genuinely meaningful when one reads and is immersed in the play as if it were a strange fiction. And indeed it is. 'Essence of death' is the climax of the Quest that the play seeks to achieve and is to be distinguished from 'visual suspension of death' as though death confesses to its masquerade as sovereign or absolute fear by unravelling itself in some degree, by suspending itself in some degree, to lay bare – however imperfectly, however inconclusively – an essence that is other than fear, that is *not* to be feared.

Fear of death may hold a corrupt culture in thrall. And yet there is a moment when this deterrent or weight of persuasion may crack. If that moment can be seized or understood the doomed culture, at the heart of its dread, begins to reach out to a new undreamt-of order of life beyond each sentence of death.

The 'agemo' phase, in African tradition, the play implies, may provide such a subtle crack of dawn within the festival of the god Ogun who comes to reside on the dark frontier of imagination I have attempted to outline with its 'eclipse of the word'. An alteration comes into that eclipse, as a consequence, which lightens metaphorically into 'visual suspension of death' within a dying culture or conflict of persuasions.

That lightening or complex transition into inner space (which is another way perhaps of comprehending agemo) is embodied in a realm of partial images that possess their catalyst in the charismatic character called the Professor.

It is the Professor who adopts Murano, the mute, in the midst of an agemo celebration that coincides with a lorry crash on the road and converts him into 'the dramatic embodiment of the visual suspension of death'.

Murano apparently dies and yet he lives. He is part-life, part-death, in the psyche of Ogun by which all the characters are shrouded as if Murano is a garment or costume that flits out of the god at dawn or dusk or other uncertain light, a costume that reminds them of the coming dissolution of their own corrupt cloak of social or political or economic practice. The cloak flits into memories of the road on which they ply their trade as lorry-driver or passenger tout or driver-trainee or insensible cargo or dog of fate that lies in a ditch.

Ogun would seem to be the very pre-condition of fear and corruption without which there is no arousal or decisive illumination of essence that is other than fear, that is not fear. And it is this ambivalent garment that gives the Professor his central place in the play. It is a centrality that is fragmented and which therefore relinquishes involuntarily, if not consciously, a total institutionalisation of Ogun, a total reinforcement of the god, to shed a dark savage light on officers of state who may masquerade as agents of political divinity. One such officer is a politician, another a captain of thugs, another a policeman. They are above the law, they are gods who trade in bribery and criminality. The Professor himself is ruthless, he forges driving licences, it is rumoured he has stolen from the Church (gods presumably are at liberty to steal from gods), he contrives wrecks in order to rehearse the procedures of agemo as threshold of the 'essence of death'.

Each wreck is an alchemical gold-mine and brings dangerous spiritual treasure into his hands. Most dangerous of all is Murano, supernatural treasure or mute, who is to pave the way to the execution of his adoptive master by Say Tokyo Kid, captain of thugs, in the last re-enactment of agemo in the play.

Say Tokyo stabs the Professor, takes him by surprise in fact, they are both engulfed in an involuntary tide, but in a strange way it is a form of repudiation of himself by himself that the Professor brings down on his head. It is a confession of blind fore-knowledge and a liberation into indescribable truth.

The Professor reminds one of Conrad's unscrupulous Kurtz and the mute Murano of Kurtz's mute figures nailed to palisade or wall. It is indeed an uncanny correspondence but an alteration of destiny occurs. When Kurtz dies he is overwhelmed by dread or loss of soul. When the Professor dies, on the other hand, he appears to lose all fear of death on the road, either as bringer of accident or victim of accident, and to gain his soul by dipping his hand into a bowl from which all consume or have learnt to distinguish themselves from the blind consumption of others in which they indulge. Death is a universal cheat and has to be cheated by reading its most intimate signals of exploiter and exploited. It is a shrouded vision and raises the central paradox of the play.

'One must cheat fear, by fore-knowledge', the Professor says and plunges us into that paradox. Fear needs to be cheated, corruption needs to be corrupted by a mask of higher corruption. Or is it that 'fore-knowledge' in the 'blind' and 'mute' implications of the play remains perpetually elusive?

> PROF: And you brought no revelation for me? You found no broken words where the bridge swallowed them?
> SAMSON: How could we think of such a thing Professor?
> PROF: A man must be alert in each event.

(p. 55)

'Fore-knowledge' may then not be a superior cheat though it comes uncannily close to it. However close, the resemblance remains open in the strangest alertness to the unexpected nature and texture of events.

The emphases upon 'blind' and 'mute' are a reconnaissance of the 'essence of death' or an equation, I would suggest, between agemo and inner space. They (those emphases) are carefully pointed within the play and they seem to me of the utmost importance in helping to sift the paradox of fore-knowledge.

How close is 'fore-knowledge' – one must ask again – to a superior cheat?

As the Professor dies he begins to discard a persona that resembles the fore-knowledge of divinity. The knife that slides into his back has the characteristics of sleight-of-hand or trick of freedom or fate and lends its weight to a bodiless mask that deceives the dying body as it slides into the essence of death. In the heart of that trick or cheat nevertheless lies a distortion that displaces anthropomorphic conceit or ruling complacent symmetry of word and gesture built into totalitarian ritual.

> PROF: You grope towards Murano, the one person in this world in whom the Word reposes.
> SAMSON: Much use is that to him. He cannot use his tongue.
> PROF: Deep. Silent but deep. Oh my friend, beware the pity of those that have no tongue for they have been proclaimed sole guardians of the Word. They have slept beyond the portals of secrets. They have pierced the guard of eternity and unearthed the Word, a golden nugget on the tongue. And so their tongue hangs heavy and they are forever silenced. Do you mean you do not see Murano has one leg longer than the other?
> SAMSON: Murano? But his legs are the same.
> PROF: Blind!
> KOTUNU: Oh I admit that he limps. Anyway he seems okay to me.
> PROF: When a man has one leg in each world, his legs are never the same. The big toe of Murano's foot – the left one of course – rests on the slumbering chrysalis of the Word. When that crust cracks my friends – you and I, that is the moment we await. That is the moment of our rehabilitation. When that crust cracks . . . (*Growing rapidly emotional, he stops suddenly, sniffs once or twice, wipes his misted glasses, returns briskly to his table.*)

> (pp. 44–5)

The above passage does foreshadow in somewhat stately emotion, I think, the coming dance of death, which is abrupt and uneven, that climaxes the play.

Such foreshadowing or fore-knowledge does court bodily tricks or resemblances to leave open inequalities of movement in the dance of the Word that hangs heavy before it drops into the soil or the road. And as it drops it resembles a new-born fool in the new, apparently innocent, dead. (No wonder many societies in the past – and not-too-distant past – were aroused by this complicity between the new-born and the new-dead to bring the dead into court, sit them up, and accuse them of crimes they had committed.)

The comic ramifications of this resemblance foreshadowing death in the new-born fool are announced quite early in the play in a scene where Samson play-acts at being the Professor. I shall quote an abridged version of this:

> ([*Samson*] *lifts the Professor's chair, dumps it on the big table and climbs on to it, leaps down almost immediately and whips the coverlet off Kotunu who stirs and slowly wakes up later. Wraps the coverlet around his shoulders and climbs back on the table. Takes out the Professor's glasses and wears them low on his nose. Puts on an imposing look and surveys a line in front of him with scorn. Breaks into a satisfied grin.*)
>
> SAMSON: E sa mi.
> SALUBI: (*down on his knees, salaams*) African millionaire!
> SAMSON: I can't hear you.
> SALUBI: Delicate millionaire!
> SAMSON: Wes matter? You no chop this morning? I say I no hear you.
> SALUBI: Samson de millionaire!
> SAMSON: Ah, my friends, what can I do for you?
> SALUBI: (*in attitude of prayer*) Give us this day our daily bribe. Amen.
> SAMSON: (*dips in an imaginary purse, he is about to fling to them a fistful of coins when he checks his hand*) Now, remember, officers first. Superintendents! (*Flings the coins. Salubi scrambles and picks up the money.*) Inspectors! (*Action is repeated.*) Sergeants! (*Again Salubi grabs the coins.*) Now that is what I call a well disciplined force. Next, those with one or two stripes . . . And now those who are new to the game . . . And good hunting friends. (*He and Salubi collapse laughing. Kotunu has sat up watching.*)
> SALUBI: Haba, make man talk true, man wey get money get power.
> SAMSON: God I go chop life make I tell true. I go chop the life so tey God go jealous me. And if he take jealousy kill me I will go start bus service between heaven and hell.
> SALUBI: Which kin' bus for heaven? . . .

SAMSON: *(reverting to his role)* Come here.

SALUBI: Yesssssssah.

SAMSON: Have you had a wash today?

SALUBI: Myself sah?

SAMSON: Open your mouth . . . go on, open your mouth. Wider! It stinks.

SALUBI: Sah?

SAMSON: It stinks. It stinks so much that I will promote you Captain of my private bodyguard. . . .

Now I want you to take the car – the long one – and drive along the Marina at two o'clock. All the fine fine girls just coming from offices, the young and tender faces fresh from school – give them lift to my house. Old bones like me must put fresh tonic in his blood.

(Busy with laughter, they do not see the Professor approach. Salubi is the first to see him, he stands petrified for some moments, then begins to stutter.)

SALUBI: Samson . . . Professor. . . !

SAMSON: What about him!

(Salubi, with trembling fingers, points in his direction, but Samson refuses to turn round.)

You think you have seen a new-born fool do you? What would Professor be doing here at this time of the day?

(As Professor gets to the door, Salubi dives under the table. Samson, too late, turns round and stares petrified. Professor is a tall figure in Victorian outfit, tails, top-hat etc., all threadbare and shiny at the lapels from much ironing. He carries four enormous bundles of newspaper and a fifth of paper odds and ends impaled on a metal rod stuck in a wooden rest. A chair-stick hangs from one elbow, and the other arm clutches a road-sign bearing a squiggle and the one word, 'BEND'.)

PROF: *(He enters in a high state of excitement, muttering to himself)* Almost a miracle . . . dawn provides the greatest miracles. . . .

(pp. 6–8)

Professor, the new-born fool, enters but fails to see himself on the stage, as it were, fails to grasp Samson's impersonation of himself and as the scene continues to unfold fails to recognise his own desk, his own chair, his own room. He dies, as it were, to everything, innocent of his own corruption, innocent of the corruption of others. As a consequence he cannot see how petrified with fear Samson and the others are at the thought of being caught by the living (or is it the dead) Professor who stands before them and how relieved they are when they sense his blindness (or involuntary simulation of death-in-life) and lead him away.

When he returns later and identifies the place at last, as if he has returned to life, he remains confused, a 'new-born fool' still, about the early morning encounter.

The entire scene needs to be considered closely in full context in order to assess the subtle weight of *partial* imagery which seems to me to inform it.

Partiality here, I think, lies in the mimicry of one by the other that brings home nevertheless how estranged each is from the other, how estranged are generations past, present and future from each other's deepest fears, and how this estrangement unites them all in base intrigue even as it reduces them to hollow self-awareness and points, in some degree, therefore, to an essence deeper than all their machinations, deeper than given appearances they uphold or mirror presented to nature.

As a consquence a hidden drama unfolds through gestures in each that mock the other in order to imply a design of truth that can never be encompassed in any model of behaviour that is susceptible – as all behaviour naturalistically is – to fear or greed or material desire.

The 'new-born fool' may give innocence a strange twist or the capacity of a sublime cheat in the theatre of death. It may provide innocence with variable masks of a clown and with the power ceaselessly to indict mimicry for the sake of mimicry, to indict theatre of violence for the sake of entertainment.

It certainly raises the question of evil, evil in the new-born, evil in the new-dead, evil in every innocent spectator fascinated with evil events.

It raises yet suspends such issues, suspends a further response to the mimicry of the new-dead fool by the new-born fool, mimicry of horrific events in new-born mirror, held up to nature, framed by complacent technology.

It suspends a response yet it does not prohibit us in a context of partial imagery, that summons our active participation, from pursuing self-critical potentials that may lie in the festival of Ogun and asking certain questions.

Do the epic gods need to be unmasked within ritual establishments as self-critical buried faculties in ourselves, and in them, on the scales of truth if one is to create a balance against their, and our, self-destructive orders or pageants of terror?

And, if so, will divine authority at the heart of human society be reborn as bearable and re-creative even as it appears to die?

For it is through perhaps a confession of evil in the agents of the gods, in humankind, that humankind may acquire the authority to judge itself in all its parts and races. The judge needs the imaginative insight to place himself or herself in the skin of the judged and to pass sentence, even sentence of death, upon the one who stands before him or her in profoundest relationship. Such authority is real. It implies an art of judgement that seeks a response, or measure of genuine self-judgement, in the judged.

Inevitably perhaps that capacity for authority and for self-judgement – such crucial revolution of sensibility – remains suspended in *The Road* but is a frontier nevertheless of illuminations that relate to shadows, or to the movement of light into dark and vice versa with variable emphases, in distinction from Conradian spectres of dread at the heart of conquest, incurable dread or totalitarian eclipse and loss of political and cultural soul.

As such the play is a considerable achievement.

I would like to add a final word on the question of the *cheat* which figures dramatically in Soyinka's play, on fear which may be cheated by a higher fear, on corruption which may be corrupted or vanquished by a higher mask of corruption in order to preserve stability or global order.

This central and open paradox of *The Road* can take us far afield. I shall confine my remarks to re-assessing the premises with which I began this article.

A long imperial age and its expansion into every culture around the globe, the movement of Capital as well as Church (both of which figure in the Professor's career), have wrought a phenomenon in that non-European writers write in European languages that dominate the globe.

That domination may evolve into a new dialogue or essential medium of consciousness within living and subtly, complexly, changing languages.

On the other hand it may seek to assert itself changelessly, so to speak, changeless domination or changeless separation, within patterns of closed tradition. And this would mean in substance that tradition lies to itself, cheats itself, when it may claim at times to accommodate the emergence of new arts – or a dialogue with ancient arts – from alien and stranger cultures. This could be particularly damaging for European innovation, African innovation, American innovation, and for post-colonial cultures thrust by history into languages that should begin to reflect a community of intentions and the evolution of startling originality that bears on the past and on the future.

The Road beyond a shadow of doubt, I think, is a highly original work within the English language. It bears on the present in that a body of tradition that reflects a cross-cultural movement and evolution of sensibility is at risk as long as societies are in thrall to absolutes (or to absolute dualisms) that seek to deceive or overcome each other by every stratagem of diabolic or military or economic technology.

In such an embattled world order of monolithic powers, or closed traditions, the cheat is enthroned until societies, on both sides of the fence, see how constricting and hopeless is the netted antagonism of dual worlds that face each other as absolutes of terror, held in check by terror each may inflict on the other, and how necessary it is to begin to conceive a third factor or entity beyond conventional fixture or polarisation, a fourth world, a fifth, a sixth, a seventh, etc., whereby the task of tradition essentially alters as it acquires complex inter-related perspectives beyond sovereign fear into passion or marvel or intricate beauty.

Such inter-relationship confirms the finiteness of all worlds, however marvellous, and yet enhances that finiteness into a window upon incalculable potentials of shared self-creation and self-judgement stretched into futurity and undisclosed numbers in order to distance the creative self from an ego of conquest that has ruled in every sphere of activity for long centuries.

1 Wole Soyinka, *The Road* (Oxford University Press, 1965) reprinted by permission of Oxford University Press. Further references to this edition are given after quotations in the text.

This essay originally appeared in *Explorations* (Dangaroo Press, 1981).

Soyinka the Tiger

NADINE GORDIMER

For me, Wole Soyinka's vision and life stand between these two statements; his own:

'A tiger doesn't have to proclaim his tigritude.'

'The man died.'

The first made graphic, with the poetic wit and impatience of one who was himself a young interpreter, the concept of négritude that Jean-Paul Sartre, with a French philosopher's distancing analysis, defined as 'the low ebb in a dialectic progression. The theoretical and practical assertion of white supremacy is the thesis; négritude's role as an anti-thetical value is the negative stage. But this negative stage will not satisfy the Negroes who are using it, and they are well aware of this. They know that they are aiming for human synthesis or fulfilment in a raceless society. Négritude is destined to destroy itself; it is the path and not the goal, the means but not the end.'

The second statement came to Soyinka as he was looking for a title for his account of his imprisonment; came as a bald statement made in reply to an enquiry about the whereabouts of another prisoner. *The man died*: last word on the matter. The end. But for Soyinka it is the opening sentence. Neither for personal safety nor peace of mind has he ever been content to step over the body, let it lie. In his books and in his life he has gone after the death-dealers among us and in ourselves. His revelations live.

For the tiger-writer who joyously flung the *innateness of black* before the theorists, Soyinka is a sophisticate whose making free of the tricks and techniques of European literature is seen by some as a contradiction. I have heard him criticised by black writers for being too difficult to be read by ordinary black people; you must understand, there is an uneasy conflict among us, in Africa, between the genuine and determined desire to extend the mind-opening pleasures of literature to millions who have had to regard these as the privilege of an elite, and the sure knowledge that you stunt and stultify that literature, to the millions' eventual depri-vation, if you ask writers to limit complexity of thought, reduce vocabulary, trim codes of reference to some supposedly accessible common denominator of comprehension.

Who is to decide whether, when Soyinka sees a beauty as a Modigliani (in one of his novels), matching her to paintings he knows and his reader in a Nigerian village, in Harare, Nairobi or Soweto, doesn't, that reader may not be curious to discover what such a painting makes of a woman, and seek out a reproduction of the long-necked ladies in a library? Why shouldn't he or she have the opportunity to look into the world through the eyes of a painter never heard of before? Is the scaling-down of complexity, vocabul-ary, reference, etc. itself not a form of perpetuating elitism? I think of myself as a young African reader, even though white, from a home where there weren't many books, learning the meaning of words from entranced reading of their contexts in books from the local library. Perhaps it simply has to be accepted that Wole's novels and poems will not be read by comic-book literates or even by white devotees of Dick Francis.

His plays, of course, are a different story. Or rather the same story (every writer is actually telling one long story put together serially in her/his works) told in a medium where comprehension by no means depends on words alone. Here, through a pantheon of well-known gods (well-known to his own Nigerians yet related to the gods of others through the mythic powers humans everywhere invest in deities in order to explain the fears and mysteries of life) Soyinka may not only have found a multiple language – words, body-movement, music – through which ideas are widely compre-hended. He also comes closer to the duty of 'interpreter to collective consciousness' that Lucien Goldmann cited as the dis-tinctive sign of great writing. There is all the difference in the world between 'writing down' to the people, and finding the imaginative power to draw upon their roots – what they *know*, what has formed the philosophy practised unconsciously in their daily life – and making these explicit in combination with the drama of the present. In South Africa, Soyinka's plays certainly have influenced black playmakers to encompass mythology (which includes historical figures of resistance to white domination become mythic) in the popular modes of people acting out their own contemporary lives.

Throughout Soyinka's novels, too, the gods are present, whether as wild Id or transcendent Superego. And here he has claimed for African literature a dimension almost lost to other literatures: where are the gods, God, the Holy Trinity, Jehovah, Mohammed et al, present in other fiction? With the exception of, perhaps, Isaac Bashevis Singer – and his were spirits rather than gods, no Jehovah himself, heaven forbid – and the tragic instance of Salman Rushdie and Mohammed, the gods and their holy cohorts are not part of the cast of fiction. With art and not didacticism, Soyinka has shown that what was overlaid in the African psyche by colonists' religions and philosophies has neither to be abandoned in the modern world to which Africa is irrevocably committed nor to result in a return to tribalism, but may merge with – as part of – modern consciousness, just as modern consciousness draws upon various other systems of thought and their personification. The creation myth of Ogun *belongs* in the world system of human thought. Soyinka's western-educated young men and women carry these gods within them, as the thinking of western non-Africans unconsciously carries Sophocles, Christ, Descartes etc. The only difference – the big one – is that the non-Africans have no knowledge of the icons of African thought, while Africans such as Soyinka have taken the opportunity to absorb the religious, philosophical and political icons of the West.

It is one of the ironies of the situation between oppressor and oppressed that while black intellectuals have appropriated the culture of whites, whites – even those living in Africa – have not taken the opportunity to appropriate the culture of blacks. They have preferred to denigrate it, relegate it to anthropology, or, at best, regard it patronisingly as a quaint anachronism in modern life. The imaginative power in Wole Soyinka's fiction, because it is conceived in modes of sophistication recognised by whites on an intellectual level familiar to them, has made the elements of African culture part of that level of world culture.

If it is a lesson, it is also a gift.

Soyinka has been able to bestow the gift because as a writer he is a romantic; whether directed, in his long writing life, to the British, the civil-war-lords or the Cocoa Cartel, his prose is full-blown, high-voltage with emotion, and taps responses left inert as much by bald didactics as by nuance. This is the Blakean tiger, whose eyes burn through the night of prejudiced indifference; no need to proclaim himself in any other way.

Sartre was wrong. The white supremacists are no longer too sure of their 'supremacy'. I speak from South Africa . . . Négritude has not destroyed itself; it changed first into Black Consciousness, a useful political tool, and then into extremist political sects like APLA (armed wing of the Pan Africanist Congress). Such formations, I stress, differ from other armies of the liberation struggle such as Umkhonto weSizwe of the African National Congress, in that the former do not accept that there comes a stage in the struggle when it takes the form of negotiation in a political climate where *the struggle itself* has established that the needs of the oppressed *come first*. For black writers, négritude (a term that means nothing to many young ones) has become the acceptance of African values in the canon of world consciousness they have done much to bring about. As for mutation into 'human synthesis . . . in a raceless society', in South Africa – the society where, Soyinka has said, the experience of oppression has been the most dire – at least the ideal is something the principal liberation alliance around the ANC envisages in a new constitution.

What has Wole Soyinka meant to fellow African writers through the experiences of a changing Africa? We in Africa are alive to assessment of ourselves by ourselves; how the literature we are making is developing, what directions it takes, its *impasse* and its progress, whether – to move from Goldmann's dictum to that of Lukács – we are succeeding in any measure, and in our different ways and different countries of the continent, to capture the 'whole of life' in these places and situations. He has not been alone in tackling contentious themes – contentious, that is, in terms of who is making the rules, the laws; colonial powers and their avatars in post-colonial power, or black independent governments and their avatars in coup and counter-coup.

Like his great contemporary, Chinua Achebe, Wole Soyinka has challenged in his novels both the colonial oppression of Nigeria and the oppression by black leadership, the post-colonial exploitation in collaboration with corrupt locals that have often made freedom an empty word. The British; and then the black dictator or military despot: the first, in retrospect, was an easier target than the second, because, as it is conventional wisdom to acknowledge, there was a common enemy which produced a more-or-less unified loyalty in the forces of resistance. The writer might be sent to prison by the white regime, but he had the support of his whole country waiting for him outside. With the devastating event of post-independence civil war in Nigeria, an event that is being blindly followed in tragic repetition in other countries of our continent, the writer whose characters exposed corruption and cruelty of the regime that led to war stood, in his society, as an enemy within his own people – reviled and hunted by the regime and those who supported it. Soyinka did not mince his words. He was not afraid to speak of 'public clownery' as 'a special prerogative of politicians', and to name one – to give a single example – 'a self-proclaimed fascist and hatchet-man'. He publicly denounced the war and sought help abroad to join in the denunciation.

But as we know, he went further than words. He tried to stop the war. Literally with his own body, by physical intervention, attempting to take over the broadcasting station. We have had many writers in Africa who have been moved to act physically as well as write, but Soyinka is the supreme and splendid example of the writer meeting the demands of his time beyond intellectual obligations as they are generally understood. (Perhaps, in the flow of moral inspiration reversing the direction it is believed to take, north-south, someone like Václav Havel was inspired, years later, by this example, to leave plays and poetry half-written and move bodily into liberation politics.)

In prison for his actions, the tiger refused to pace the cage impotently. Soyinka wrote, he stored in memory, he drew on toilet paper what he could not write about his experiences and those of other prisoners: when he came out he compiled and published the most complete work of prison literature ever written in Africa, and – to my knowledge – written in modern times in the world. It is complete – in the truly rounded sense of the word – because the facts, the names are recorded with an authority of meticulous observation and bold retention in this chapter of the Book of The Dead our continent is continuing to compile even now, with horrors published blandly in reports of United Nations' observers – but also because it includes the brilliantly written reflections of a fine mind triumphantly lucid under unspeakable duress. *The Man Died* is, in a very real and strange sense, the victory of art over all the forces of philistinism. We are inclined to forget that these include hatred and cruelty.

Wole has written his own biography. We, in appraising his wonderful work and life so far, cannot attempt to compete with the inside story; only to provide some modest footnotes. He once wrote a poem: 'THREE WHITE HAIRS! frail invaders of the under-growth/ interpret time. I view them, wired wisps, vibrant-coiled/ beneath a magnifying glass, milk-thread presages.' The last time I saw him (Los Angeles, a couple of years ago) the presage had come to pass: there were many white hairs in that impressive head whose hair he had described as once being 'Hirsute hell chimney-spouts, black thunderfloes'. If the tiger's coat was changing markings, he himself was unchanged, except in the sense of responding with the same energy to new demands of our continent. He has never spared African writers – including, of course, himself – in continuing assessment of where they are wanting in ability and will to resist (as he phrased it in 1967 but which surely holds good for his sixtieth year) submission of 'integrity to the monolithic stresses of the time'. He has never done the disappearing act away from Africa into the shelter of world literature that comes with the Nobel Prize, although his presence at the innumerable conferences held on Af. Lit. often has been more a matter of anticipation than realisation . . . and I confess my disapproval of this no-show has changed to fellow-feeling since I find myself in his same situation, under the laurel wreath that brings about demand in excess of the supply of time!

Where freedom is absent, politics is fate.[1]

Freedom is still absent in Africa: withheld by the exploitation of corrupt governments, neo-colonialism, the misery of civil wars and economic chaos. And fate – in whatever form history shapes it – has been the subject of story-tellers since they began to record time in terms of human lives, inventing the art of narrative. It's not without significance that the site of withdrawal in indifference to the state of society is called the Ivory Tower. Isn't ivory itself the poached tusks of elephants, the profits of exploitation of an African resource, a fit symbol of tranquillity and comfort gained, anywhere and everywhere in the world, by the plunder of the lives of others?

No wonder African writers don't inhabit the Tower. Commitment is our natural habitat. Like the savannah, the forest, the veld, the desert, the squatter camp, the cities crowded with slumped figures of the unemployed, the ghetto and the once-white suburb. But commitment doesn't make art; our writers have to be disabused of that illusion. The writer in Africa has to *make art out of commitment*. Soyinka is a prototype of that writer. The tall man from the North casts his outline down Africa, South, East and West, tracing a literature that makes many sacrifices to society but does not sacrifice the integrity of art – imagination, beauty, illumination, celebration of life.

1 Irving Howe.

Wole Soyinka and a Living Dramatist: a Playwright's Encounter with Soyinka's Drama

FEMI OSOFISAN

I

Why was I selected as one of those to write an essay to commemorate Soyinka's birthday? And why did I accept?

If these questions seem curious, the circumstances should explain. For, as it must be well known by now, I have been one of Soyinka's ardent critics, to whom he himself has replied with some of his now famous diatribes. I have subjected to serious questioning both his aesthetics and the underlying philosophy of his historical interpretations, especially in such essays as 'Anubis Resurgent' and 'Ritual and the Revolutionary Ethos'. Indeed, some of my works – of which *No More the Wasted Breed* is an obvious example – were written precisely to plead an opposing point of view to Soyinka's, in a conscious aim to contest some of his stated positions.

Soyinka himself, who is not known to leave any criticism unanswered, has come down thunderingly in response to this challenge, replying in such caustic essays as 'Who's Afraid of Elesin Oba?', and 'The Critic and Society: Barthes, Leftocracy and other Mythologies', most of which have been collected now in a book appropriately titled, *Art, Dialogue and Outrage*!

So – why me? The answer of course is simple. By inviting me to make a contribution here, to this commemorative occasion, the editor must have discerned correctly a fact that may not always be apparent – that all our quarrels with Soyinka are, in the end, nothing less than a tribute to his genius; that our disagreements with him represent, with all their fierceness, the kind of homage that admirers pay to masters.

43

In this regard, perhaps the best way to explain the relationship will be to illustrate with an analogous incident, and recall here the answer that André Gide, the famous novelist, was reported to have given when asked to name the greatest poet France has produced. 'Victor Hugo, of course,' he replied spontaneously. And then added, '*Hélas!*'

It is the same ambiguous tribute that we pay, artists of my generation, to Wole Soyinka. For without dispute, Soyinka is today the greatest living African dramatist – *alas!* Like the great Hugo, Soyinka stands in the world of letters like a giant elephant, massive in his productivity, and colossal in his artistic vision. Endlessly fertile and endlessly inventive, he has also been active in all the literary genres, as well as on the print and the electronic media which were, perhaps fortunately, not available to Hugo. But like the French poet, Soyinka has proven on different occasions to be just as equally venomous with his foes, and as unsparing in his devastation of opponents, almost as if petulance were an inseparable twin of genius.

Certainly both writers share the relish, akin sometimes to puerile glee, of sparring with people that others would dismiss as minions. Fierce democrats both of them in their ideals, and intolerant of tyrannical power, they are nevertheless surprisingly aristocratic in their tastes and demeanours. And again, like Hugo, Soyinka reveals himself to be a rigid moralist, but with a paradoxical, abundant penchant for the sensual, if not even the hedonistic.

Nevertheless the reservation with which we qualify Soyinka's talent is not exactly the same as Hugo's. Our great countryman may have been as equally prolific and versatile, but he is never nearly as profligate with words and sentiment. And if he has similarly experimented with a rich diversity of forms and techniques, in which his personality and his personal emotions are deeply implicated, he has so far succeeded in doing so with much less evidence of the occasional superfluous flamboyance, the embarrassing sentimentality, or the self-indulgent laxity of some of Hugo's works.

The 'alas' we attach to Soyinka is different from Hugo's, indeed, because it refers more to his audience, than to his achievement. For clearly, he is a man out of his time. He is a splendid and talented playwright, but one who is seldom produced; a brilliant writer in a land without readers; a politician at home and at ease in no political organisation; a dreamer on a raft commanded by cannibal louts; a visionary at a time when the people's heroes are the harlots and philistines, Soyinka, the dramatist, is encountered more on the pages of his books, that is, more frequently in the libraries and classrooms, than on the platforms of the stage. Since we live in a country in which illiteracy is rampant therefore, it is not chimeric or mischievous to suggest that a man like Soyinka would have been unknown, at least among our people, were it not for his other activities, his noisy and fearless interventions in our political life. For a writer of such skill and profundity, this kind of situation is nothing less than scandalous, if not even tragic. And it is certainly one of the factors that have contributed to shaping the contours of the relationship I am going to speak about.

Partly because of all this therefore, my treatment of the subject here today is going to lean heavily on the personal, and the anecdotal. I say partly, because there is also of course the other concern to avoid irrelevance. Soyinka's work has already accumulated a vast and comprehensive list of critical studies, with innumerable diverse approaches, to which it would be hard to add without a risk of tedious repetition.

However, since I regard this occasion as a celebration, we can afford for once to shun the usual pedantic intellection, in favour of an informal approach which might otherwise be condemned as subjective. Drawing from my unique intimacy with both the man and his works, my aim will be to narrate as clearly as possible the fiction of an epoch and a relationship, to deal with a dimension of Soyinka that has not been much discussed, that is, his influence on us, the younger generation after his; to expound on what he has meant to us as a model artist and political activist; and explain why, and how, we have had to deconstruct this idol in the end, in order to clear the way to our own maturation. It is a story that I have begun before on other occasions, but perhaps the moment has come at last, on this sixtieth birthday, to stand back, and let the story tell itself.

*

II

In 1946 then, the year that I was born, Wole Soyinka left the Government College, Ibadan (or, 'GCI' as the school was, and is still, popularly called). And thirteen years afterwards, when in 1959 I was admitted into the same school, Soyinka returned from his university studies in Leeds and London to begin his theatrical activities at the University of Ibadan, where I myself would study and later launch my own theatre career. It means therefore that a lot of circumstances have linked our careers right from the onset, and that his influence and example were to be significant in my own development.

Certainly before I encountered his theatre, I was already familiar, and enamoured, with the name. His plays had been produced in February 1959 at the University Arts Theatre, by Geoffrey Axworthy and Ken Post, but I was too young then to know about these, and too far away in my little remote village of Ifo, even to have heard about them. But when I came to Ibadan, Soyinka's name was on everybody's lips on account of his prodigious activities on the stage and at the Mbari Club in Adamasingba, on the other side of town. I remember buying a copy of *A Dance of the Forests* sometime in the early sixties, and not understanding a word of it. But for me at that time, this impenetrability only made the work more impressive, for it went to confirm further the depth and magnitude of the author's talent. And when I then read Chris Okigbo's poetry, and met the same wall of mystery and incomprehension, I was doubly impressed. Art was obviously so profound an experience, that it could not, and should never, be conveyed in simple, accessible syntax. And, thus inspired, I struggled to write my own passionate imitations, based on the principle that lucidity was a crime, and that true genius expressed itself only through complex private codes and esoteric metaphors.

Then one night, through a special arrangement at our school, a number of us were driven to the university campus several kilometres away, to watch the revues collectively entitled *Before the Blackout*. And I recollect being thrilled, but disappointed. I was captivated by the fierce satirical portraits that Soyinka drew of well-known public figures, especially at that period in mid-1965, when the horrors of our politics were beginning to escalate. In particular, two sketches – the *Ogbugbu of Gbu*, denouncing opportunistic leadership; and *For Better for Worse*, with the two ministers tied back to back and resolving to 'dissolve the people' – remained memorable in my mind. But still, I felt that this was in the end only juvenile work; that the great Soyinka that I had read about was merely indulging himself, prostituting his talents. And to cap the disappointment of the night, we were not able, as we had hoped so fervently, even to catch a glimpse of the great man himself.

The main thing that left an impression however, was the Arts Theatre stage itself. It was simply fascinating. I found it totally different, and much superior in its possibilities, from the crude stage we used at the GCI, even despite the improvements brought there by our theatre-loving principal, Derek Bullock, who initiated us into the art, and never missed a year without directing a major school play. And this impression about the Arts Theatre grew firmer when, a few months afterwards, we were again taken there to watch the production of *Kongi's Harvest*.

Now, this new play was a completely different experience from *Before the Blackout*, or from anything we had done on our stage at the GCI. *The Blackout* had been merely amusing, prankish, mischievous. But this one was totally mesmerising. I was entranced by the scenic effects, by the costuming, the play of lights and colours, the dancing, the music. I had never seen anything like this. It brought back to sight the splendour of a world that was once ours but which we had lost; it recalled even to my young and fragile mind the poetry of my people's original essence. I felt transported, ennobled; I was thoroughly soaked in the play's spectacular universe; I didn't want it to end. For the very first time in my whole experience, I felt the surge of primordial energies, the currents of magical entrancement associated anciently with drama; and the evening was like an initiation into the secrets of what true African theatre should be.

It is perhaps important to stress here that what captivated me then about Soyinka's drama, and which was to be so significant with regard to my own development, was not so much the *message* of the play, as rather the mechanics of performance, the persuasive brilliance of the acting, the seductiveness of the successive spectacles, and the rich explorations of language deployed in the dialogue. *Kongi's Harvest* is striking in its use of contrasts: remarked in the interpolation of strong characters, with their verve and humour, such as Oba Danlola and Sarumi, with weak but no less compelling figures, such as the comic marionettes of the Reformed Aweri Fraternity, or the simple-looking but pragmatic Dende; the simultaneous or alternating shifts of setting and scenery, from spartan prison yard to sumptuous palace, to Segi's nightclub, to Kongi's sombre mountain retreat; the rich panoply of costumes ranging from the colourful traditional robes of Danlola and his retinue to the khaki drills of Kongi's Carpenters' Brigade; and so on. Spectacle alternated smoothly with moments of dark caricature; the electric caves of tension yielded to the open planes of laughter and celebration; the exuberant, ribald scenes of harvest succeeded those of keen conspiracies or of sophist meditation.

And above all, the dance, the music and the proverb-enriched dialogue. These, to my young mind then, were the real plums of the evening. We had been brought up tamely as Christians, raised through a regular colonial education modelled after the British curricula, with its staple diet of culture based on the notion that all 'literature' was written, that all drama was primarily a text, that theatre achieved its quintessence in the age and the opus of Shakespeare. English was the language of civilisation and, in GCI especially, to stray even for a second into 'the vernacular' was a venal sin that was immediately sanctioned. Hence the last acquaintance with our traditional culture that any of us remembered at all belonged to a remote past, to the time before we came to Ibadan, to the primary school days when we stole away from home to follow the masquerades.

But now, in the play of Wole Soyinka, all that past was suddenly there again, asserting its beauty, its lyric tones. It gave vitality to a stage hitherto inert; and validity to the culture we had been taught was non-existent or primitive and pagan. Theatre was no longer Shakespeare alone any more, or Shaw, it was now also Soyinka. And we noticed that although he used the English language throughout in his dialogues, it never once struck us as incongruous or implausible, even when the speaker was the illiterate Dende or the rustic Sarumi. Particularly in those moments of tragic grandeur, the spoken words seemed to merge superbly with drum and movement and song, and the dance unfurled itself in a diction mellowed by invocative metaphors:

DRUMMER:
> This is the last
> That we shall dance together
> They say we took too much silk
> For the royal canopy
> But the dead will witness
> We never ate the silkworm . . .

DANLOLA: (*comes forward, dancing softly*)
> This is the last
> Our feet shall touch together
> We thought the tune
> Obeyed us to the soul
> But the drums are newly shaped
> And stiff arms strain
> On stubborn crooks, so
> Delve with the left foot
> For ill-luck; with the left
> Again for ill-luck; once more
> With the left alone, for disaster
> Is the only certainty we know.

These invocations of the ancestors, these verses filled with echoes of *oriki* and *ijala*, spoke straight to a yearning nostalgia, to the hitherto dormant ventricles of ancestral memory, an area of ourselves we thought was dead. Soyinka had found the ingenious solution of making his English indigenous to the listening ear, in such a way that his characters still retained their authenticity, and the locus of action remained identifiably African. For those of us already interested in writing, *Kongi's Harvest* had opened the way and provided a model, which we discussed over and over again when we returned to our dormitories.

III

The following year, just as I was entering into the university in Ibadan, the civil war began, after the months of mass murder and arson in the west, the abortive coup d'état by Major Nzeogwu and his friends, and the flagitious pogroms in the north directed primarily at Igbos. The Mbari Club closed down; figures like Ulli Beier and Geoffrey Axworthy departed from Ibadan; Okigbo fled to the east, where he was soon to perish on the battlefront; Clark, seriously implicated in the coup attempt as we heard, went into hiding; and Soyinka was sent by Gowon into detention for undisclosed reasons. In those despondent years we tried to sustain artistic life through our activities in such groups as the Orisun Theatre, the troupe founded by Wole Soyinka and now run, in a touching gesture of defiance to the regime in Lagos, by Dapo Adelugba; the Students' Dramatic Society, of which I twice became the president; the Armchair Theatre founded and run by Paul Worika; and others. But these were mainly middling achievements: with Soyinka's exit, it was as if the lights had literally been lowered on the stage.

But then he returned, at the end of the war, to his post as head of the Department of Theatre in Ibadan, and for a while, the old glamour returned. My very first meeting with him took place at last, shortly before I took the decision to return to the campus for postgraduate studies. Later, in 1971, I finally achieved one of my ambitions, when I was taken into the cast of *Madmen and Specialists*, and had the chance of acting under Soyinka's direction, alongside his famous actors.

I was fulfilling a long-held ambition, but paradoxically in fact, this was where my apprentice adoration began to ebb, and my questioning of Soyinka's aesthetics started. As I saw it then, Soyinka was not a good director at all. Unlike the meticulous, painstakingly watchful Axworthy, for whom I had acted a few years earlier in an adaptation of one of Henshaw's plays, Soyinka would concede only the most minimal clues to guide the actor along. That would have been all appropriate, I thought, for a cast of experienced, professional actors, and for a script that was easy to understand. But when we read *Madmen* at the first rehearsals, none of us could say what it was about. And to the questions of those of us who dared to ask – for the experienced ones, weaned to Soyinka's methods, had learnt to keep their bafflement to themselves, or express it only in self-mocking exchanges behind his back – all Soyinka would volunteer was that we should be patient, and let the meaning come to us. For me, new to the cast and to the director, and yet anxious to prove myself, those weeks of rehearsals were nothing less than sheer torment.

What saved me in the end, to confess now, was the genius of the late Femi Johnson, perhaps the best actor, along with Jimi Solanke, that our theatre in English has produced. He did not know of course, but it was him I watched all the while, and tried to emulate as he diligently ploughed through his role and grew stupendously into the character of Aafa, the epileptic leader of the mendicants. It is not an experience, unfortunately, that one can easily capture in words. OBJ, as we fondly called him, would probably earn his merit one day as a determining factor in the shaping of Soyinka's dramaturgy, for he was an actor born for strong roles, and for whom Soyinka undoubtedly created those protean, histrionic figures always at the centre of his cast. OBJ built up the role of Aafa, and achieved such astounding metamorphoses, especially in those moments of his fits, that his achievement became both an actor's paradigm and a direct personal challenge. As Blindman, I knew I had to try to match his performance, or ruin the play. And I believe that all the rest of the cast felt the same way.

But, in the end, Soyinka was right: the meaning of the play did come to us, without his explanation. *Madmen*, as most people know now, is not a conventional play. It does not narrate a story as such; its main purpose, instead, is to narrate a historical *situation*, one that is macabre, and immensely frightening, by animating it with graphic and telling illustrations. Its goal is not catharsis therefore, but rather, shock and psychic wounding; an attempt to confront the audience with its own mirror of horror, to immerse it in the excretions of its own prevailing brutalities, the sanious nightmare of its *condition humaine*. Hence you could not say what the play was *about*, only what it did to your psyche and to your mind. You could not summarise it; you could only *experience* it! Soyinka's intention, as far as I understood it, was to rouse the audience to the savage atrocities of the war and the inhumanity of the war leaders, perhaps with the hope of provoking a collective guilt that would lead ultimately to the demand for cleansing and atonement.

I had fulfilled a dream, but my inner questions had begun; and instead of exultation, I was discovering a new torment. For, as I soon discovered, not many in the audience had caught the play's meaning. Certainly they enjoyed our performance, and had been sufficiently captivated to stay through to the end of it. But still, they demanded – what was the play about? As actors we had had a privileged access no doubt into the play's disturbing universe, since we had had weeks to grow into it, grow with it, and ingest it. But the audience which comes to Soyinka's play, without the benefit of such long contemplation, cannot but leave confused. And the question is, why should such a consummate artist, with such a mastery of the theatre's resources, be content to leave this swampy distance between himself and his audience?

The actor in me had attained a fulfilment, but for the part of me that was budding playwright, I had arrived only at the crossroads of nascent puzzles. Now inevitably the point was slowly growing in my mind, that to reach the audience, to make some kind of telling impact, stagecraft was not enough; that the playwright, in order to be relevant, had to reach further than visual and auditory hypnosis, and commit himself. The techniques of a modern ritual, such as those resumed glibly into the name of 'absurd theatre', would fascinate, but not inform or challenge our audience. And 'information' and lucidity were important, and vital, because our people were at a crucial juncture of history, at which all the options must be stripped naked, for decisions were waiting to be taken on whether we would forever remain victims, or recover, in Cabral's words, 'the upward paths of our history'. In fulfilment of such objectives, it seemed to me, although still only fleetingly, a new aesthetics, different from Soyinka's, would have to be created.

It is possible, I am sure, that anyone reading this would be tempted to smile at that last statement, recalling that, as everyone knows, 'Soyinka's aesthetics' is not just one uniform, monolithic thing, but quite a diversity of styles. But if I use the term out of apparent, familiar error, it is because the dramaturgical style which is most frequently identified with Soyinka is the one observed in such plays as *Madmen*. In truth, this oblique technique is only employed, with significant variations, in just about three out of his vast corpus of plays – namely, *A Dance of the Forests*, *Madmen* itself, and especially, *The Road*. In all the other plays – *The Trials of Brother Jero*, *The Strong Breed*, *The Swamp Dwellers*, *The Lion and the Jewel*, etc – Soyinka's style is limpid and clear, and his meaning quite straightforward.

Nevertheless, with Soyinka, those easy plays are not usually considered to be his 'serious' plays, but rather, like those a playwright such as the late Anouilh would label his 'amusements'. Certainly these plays do not carry the weighty themes that are known to be Soyinka's most passionate obsessions – such, for instance, as the wanton and cynical abuse of political power in Africa, the rampant corruption, the erosion of individual freedom, the elusive meaning of history, or the exploration of the mythology of death. Or if they treat any of such subjects, it is mainly with an air of levity, in an atmosphere of grand burlesque, with the playwright portraying his villains with ribald indulgence as delightful, rascally tricksters whose exploits we even enjoy.

But with *Madmen*, I began to see that the real problem with Soyinka's theatre was, and is, not so much its 'obscurity', but rather its ambiguity, its refusal, after many scenes of candid exposure, to proclaim a formal stand in the conflict it ceaselessly enacts between the forces of evil and of good, of death and life. Therefore, examined from this basic perspective, it becomes superfluous to draw a line between his 'serious' and 'lighter' plays, for all are linked by this primordial bridge of ideological ambiguity. Between a play like *The Lion and the Jewel* and, say, *Death and the King's Horseman*, or between *The Road* and *Requiem for a Futurologist*, or even *The Bacchae of Euripides* and *Opera Wonyosi*, the fundamental thematic impulse is 'constant' – namely, that there seems to be a continual, restless swing (once identified by Biodun Jeyifo as an *aporia*) between on the one hand a sincere and passionate quest for modernising impulses and, on the other, a loving celebration of the exotic tropes of tradition; between a mordant censure of the destructive rituals of megalomania, and a simultaneous fascination for the masques of regal institutions and feudalist structures. This rite of antithetic self-revising, if one might call it so, left me baffled for a long while, until it came to clarify itself much later on, in my consciousness, as a potentially fatal flaw to a vocation of revolutionary commitment.

IV

After Ibadan, I left for France, and coincidentally, Soyinka himself left Nigeria that same year on what was to prove a long exile abroad. It was in his car that, coming from London, I first drove to Paris, then to Bonn and Koln, and then to Brussels. He was to settle to a life of wandering now, more or less, as he embarked on his angry post-war memoirs, the proofs of which I sometimes helped to correct. But what was to be most helpful to me was the opportunity that his frequent passage through Paris afforded me to meet, and sometimes watch at work, such theatre luminaries as Peter Brook, Robert Wilson (of *Le regard des sourds*), and most important of all, Jean-Marie Serreau, founder of the black troupe called the Théâtre de la Tempête, which had been responsible for the Parisian premières of the plays of Kateb Yacine and Aimé Césaire. Through Serreau, already ill then and prematurely dying, and through his actors, I came to be introduced to the marvellous world of the Cartoucherie, and especially to the iconoclastic, renovative productions of Ariane Mnouchkine and her 'extended family'. Once also, at a festival of the Théâtre des Nations presided over by the legendary Jean-Louis Barrault, I participated in a French production of excerpts from *A Dance of the Forests* with Alton Kamalo, Jimi Solanke and Daniel Maximim, directed by Soyinka himself.

I mention these details simply to show how close I was to Soyinka and to his influence, at a time when my experience of theatrical aesthetics was rapidly expanding, maturing in a tangent direction to his, and hence to underline how traumatic it was going to be when I had to break from him. Our friendship was growing, which was a unique and really remarkable thing, when you know how closely Soyinka guards his privacy, and almost spontaneously erects fences between himself and strangers. Once in, once admitted into this private world, you discover behind the withdrawn or intimidating façade a surprisingly warm and tender personality, a fastidiously caring companion, full of humour and anecdote, of compassion and healthy mischief. But unfortunately, it is also a personality for whom friendship is precariously fragile. Haunted by its accumulation of laurels, spoiled perhaps by success and repeatedly proven accomplishment, it tends to view the slightest criticism as pugnacious challenge, and especially when coming from a friend, as a gesture equating to treachery. The storm was coming therefore, to our relationship.

Paris had helped clear my eyes. I had concluded that, in order to construct an aesthetics and a theatrical practice more suited to our generation's needs, I would need to borrow from Soyinka's fertile store, from his knowledge of stage mechanics for instance, but at the same time go further forward from where he stopped, to an unambiguous luminosity; that my own journey through the stage would have to fulfil itself along a map that was yet to be written, and which nobody but myself could script. And romantically, I thought I knew where I needed to locate myself – in those areas precisely where Soyinka's dramaturgy was silent, or hazy, or furtive, the symbolic province of his repeatedly advanced, and repeatedly unclarified 'Third Force'.

Let me explain. In virtually all of Soyinka's plays – and there have been seventeen published to date, each marking a substantial achievement – two major 'forces' at least are always clear and unambiguously in conflict. There are first the Ogunnian protagonists, those who stand for strength and virility, for fecundity, sexuality, voluptuousness. They are the ones who defend the right to life and joy, who embody in themselves the principles of both creativity and destructiveness, of nobility mingled with rascality and of a truculent, nature-enhancing promiscuity. They are 'Ogunnian', because the playwright deliberately casts them in the mould which he himself has continuously claimed for Ogun, the Yoruba god of iron, patron of poets and warriors – that is, as alloys of contradictory essences, both positive and negative, and as the central protagonists in a dangerous drama involving the very survival of their communities. They are called Danlola, or Dionysos, or Baroka, or Jero, or Elesin Oba, or even Sebe Irawe, and sometimes they are endowed with visionary power, sometimes with questionable, criminal attributes, but always with the gift of the gab and love of impersonation. They are superb talkers, irrepressible histrions: their articulateness is almost synonymous with, and symbolic of, their fecund prowess. The playwright feeds their mouths exuberantly with his most mellifluous metaphors, sings their slightest gestures in loquacious trope. Against them are the 'opposite people', the men of order or sterility, of emptiness and parsimony. They are the demagogues like Kongi or Pentheus or Emperor Boky, men maimed by the obsession with power, and the playwright rises to his satirical climax in the scenes where he caricatures their empty, vulgar lust.

Of course it would be gross misinterpretation to suggest that Soyinka's plays are always structured along these elementary manichaean divisions, or that the conflict between such forces is his sole or permanent preoccupation. The confrontation in, *Death and the King's Horseman*, for instance, between Elesin and Pilkins, goes beyond a simple matching of good against evil, even beyond the contending logic of two cultural philosophies, and is meant to probe deeper into the metaphysical traumas of a society in transition, as well as the role of the committed individual in such rites of passage. Again, in *The Road*, Professor's schizoid personality, his demonic searching and criminality, his predatory expeditions and near cannibalistic relationship with his abject clients and road denizens, are aspects of a private necromancy, a quasi-religious quest, whose main theme is the exploration of mystic space.

But this example of *The Road* leads me, in fact, to the last point I wish to make about Soyinka's drama and its significance for me and my contemporaries. This is the fact that, no matter how strongly drawn the principal characters may be, they are always surrounded by a third group of actors, who may be less eloquent, but are not for all that less noisy, and are, interestingly, always numerous. These are the common people, the downtrodden, the victims, the outcasts. As layabouts, thugs and touts in *The Road*; crippled mendicants in *Madmen*; market women in *Death and the King's Horseman*; citizens, palace attendants, or official thugs in *Kongi's*

Harvest; or common prisoners in *From Zia with Love*, they serve as foil or fodder for the chief protagonists, and also for the playwright's simulated rituals. They are the ones who keep the stage alive and vibrant, recreate for us the graphic tableaux of succeeding narrations, fill the play with mime and song, dance and ribaldry, and generally sustain our attention in the margin of the plays' wonderland. Indeed, they are the characters who make Soyinka's plays a boon to actors and directors, who make plausible David Cook's fervid contention that the plays, far from being esoteric, are 'potentially popular'. But Cook of course misses the real point of the argument, as we found out without any surprise when, in 1991, I decided to mount a production of *The Road* at the Arts Theatre. It was easy naturally to dissolve the fears of those who had only previously encountered the play in print, and concluded from their reading that the play was totally inaccessible. Even my cast began from such prejudices, until the play asserted its histrionic power, and surprised them with the richness of its theatrical possibilities. Soyinka is not for reading, but for staging, for performance. His plays abound in spectacle and movement and colour; in multiple settings, flashbacks and dramatic re-enactments; in characters made exotic and compelling by their eloquence and laughter, their gift for improvisation and mimicry. Enhanced by the use of lighting and sound effects, the presence of skilful singers and dancers, the lyrical power of the language, Soyinka's plays cannot but be entrancing for an audience, and even more so especially, for actors Cook can sit back therefore and smile.

But in fact, this is where that initial fundamental question again rears its head, because, simply, the ingenuity of stagecraft does not unfortunately translate automatically into a clarity of meaning. A successful production of *The Road* could turn it into an actor's delight, into even the favourite of the most fastidious of theatre-goers, but it would not for all that, if the director remained faithful to the text, make its meaning less ambiguous. So what reading is one expected to make of these endings? When a play on a brutal tyrant ends with his opponents destroyed, and he himself ranting noiselessly into the midst of an orgiastic celebration, does the spectator come out with a feeling of hope and renewed commitment, or of melancholy, bafflement, or tragic despair? What has been gained, or lost, when Professor dies, and what does his tortured valediction mean to the lives of the layabouts, or to ours? Can David Cook answer these questions with any certainty? And why would a playwright, who himself is at the forefront of political activism, and has been made to pay dearly for it again and again by our anti-human regimes, why would such a radical playwright prefer to end his plays with these frenzied scenes of logorrhoea? Why this deliberate commingling of brilliant stagecraft and with-held resolutions?

But above all, is the playwright trying to tell us something, which we are perhaps yet to grasp, by setting up so many actors on stage, and therefore foregrounding the very fact of *acting* itself? Is it possible that we are meant to read from this the notion that history itself is an artificial construct, a circus show commanded by freaks and mountebanks; and that human destiny is mostly the invention of charlatans we cannot control or humanise? And in that case, would this preference for an existentialist open-ending therefore enhance the spectator's freedom, or merely problematise it? For a playwright in a hurry, eager to kick history awake, I could only be suspicious of, and impatient with such uncertainties. As I freed myself of Soyinka's influence, and began to struggle with my own demons, it occurred to me that in *A Dance of the Forests*, Soyinka had probably forespoken his dramaturgical choices himself, when he created Forest Head, the character which, interestingly enough, he himself played in the first (and so far, the only) production that he directed in 1960. Forest Head, like a great theatre director or manager, assembles an enormous cast for his 'dance', shuttling adventurously across time spaces and across generations, and summoning actors from the past and future for his restorative scenes. But as he stands back to watch his scheme unfold, we hear him suddenly confess, as follows:

. . . The fooleries of beings whom I have fashioned closer to me weary and distress me. Yet I must persist, *knowing that nothing is ever altered*. My secret is my eternal burden – to pierce the encrustations of soul-deadening habit, and bare the mirror of original nakedness – knowing full well, *it is all futility*. Yet I must do this alone, *and no more*, since to intervene is to be guilty of contradiction, and yet to remain altogether unfelt is to make my long-rumoured ineffectuality complete . . . (*My italics.*)

V

It seemed to me therefore, as I began to write, that Forest Head was speaking for Soyinka, and that the deliberate ambiguities which 'conclude' his serious plays were the rhetoric of a liberal humanism which, in the context of our country, was patently luxurious. The task to do, I told myself, was now to open up that 'third' area of the stage, and bring to central focus the drama Soyinka had tucked into the margins. I made it my goal to give voice to the underlings of society and bring them to speak not as silhouettes any more, not as supporting chorus to the heroes, whether Ogunnian or otherwise, but as concrete characters speaking themselves into history, inscribing their own longings and agonies into the public script. Thus my theatre became, in a number of ways, an open dialogue with Soyinka.

But it is twenty years now since that debate began, and in spite of our plays, the conditions of our country, and the plight of the common people have continued to worsen. In 1992 Soyinka wrote and directed *From Zia with Love*, demonstrating, except for a certain slowness in pace, that little has altered in his dramaturgical emphases. The theme is still the same criminal misuse of power by the country's leadership, and the gross caricature of its avarice and megalomania, achieved through the now familiar, effervescent use of chorus-like actor-prisoners whose leader, this time, even claims to have been trained by the late veteran dramatist, Hubert Ogunde. And also, as in his earlier plays, we hear of a potential resistance to this regime, which proves abortive not only because its leadership is summarily 'wasted', but more crucially, because neither its programme nor its strategy is ever clarified for us, and everything remains mysteriously vague, hidden in the head of its leaders. We are left, like before, in the earlier plays, in the same inert circuit of frustrated dreams.

But, a few months before, inspired by the on-going agitations for democracy on our continent, and the success of some of the popular movements, like the one next door to us in the Republic of Benin, I wrote *Yungba-Yungba and the Dance Contest*, to hail the dawn of a coming new age. Directed by Sunbo Marinho for the Arts Theatre stage, the rehearsals turned into a drama of their own, as actresses increasingly became apprehensive of repression from the state. It was quite a struggle then, to carry on in the face of these palpable anxieties. But Marinho was courageous and in the end, the production proved to be such a success that it was even commissioned, in the euphoric days of the election campaigns, by an organ of the State! Sadly of course, that euphoria has again evaporated, and left the wounded nation tottering in the trauma of military legerdemain.

The debate with Soyinka is therefore not resolved, and perhaps this will prove instructive to the dramatists who are coming after us. It is a tribute to Soyinka's greatness, and a testimony of his continuing relevance, that we continue up till this moment to define our work so self-consciously against his own. And it is certainly fertilising for us that he has not ceased to create, and offer new challenges. Thirty-five years at the pinnacle of any profession is no mean feat for any individual, least of all an artist. Hopefully, therefore, the river will continue to run, and our art will never forsake its responsibility to itself, its creators, and its consumers. But it is obviously no longer a question of who is right now between us, or what is currently fashionable. In the light of events in the country and on our continent, in a post-Gorbachev era, it is simply that Eshu is 'in the ascendant'; that history has tricked both of us.

The Fiction of Wole Soyinka

ABDULRAZAK GURNAH

In the complex opening of Soyinka's *The Interpreters*, important features of the young friends who are the central figures in the narrative are established clearly. The clarity only comes with hindsight, which in itself is a dynamic mode of enquiry in the novel, as can be seen in the journey the friends make to Egbo's ancestral creek-town. Egbo returns to the creek-town to test out his response to the invitation from the elders that he should succeed his grandfather as their leader. The invitation tempts him because he 'despised the age which sought to mutilate his beginnings'.[1] The evocative language of Egbo's immersion in his past endorses his attachment to it. Yet Egbo sees the creek-town as 'an interlude from reality' and this points to his view of the paradoxical relationship between the past and his age. For Egbo both valorises the past as archetypal community and fears the demands that it will make on him. In the end, he feels the pull of the past as the pull of death:

> He acknowledged it finally, this was a place of death. And admitted too that he was drawn to it, drawn to it as a dream of isolation, smelling its archaic menace and the violent undertows, unable to deny its dark vitality. (p. 12)

In *Season of Anomy*, Ofeyi echoes Egbo's response in his view of Aiyéró, the rural community which both tempts and at first repels him. He says to Pa Ahime, one of the Aiyéró elders:

61

even the state of content can become malignant. Like indifference.
Or complacency. Already you are near stagnant . . . I don't know
how to convey to you the smell of mould, stagnation which clings to
places like this. (p. 6)[2]

Ofeyi's ambivalence is a stage in his journey to resolve the dilemma
of appropriate action in a political state ruled by terror. The
resolution is arrived at, in part, by exploring the meaning of the
rootedness represented by Aiyéró. The rural landscape is valorised
as authentic and ideal, powerfully symbolised by the silted pool in
the heart of Aiyéró. But opposed to its humane creed is the pitiless
cynicism of the Cartel. The novel debates the adequacy of humane
politics in the face of such oppression.

In *The Interpreters*, Egbo's ambivalence about the past and its
relation to the present is part of an exploration of the meaning of
tradition in post-colonial Nigeria, in some ways a less urgent but
more profound enquiry than that in *Season of Anomy*. In addition,
the mode of enquiry in the earlier novel, its narrative method,
effectively reflects the novel's structure. The flashback from the
night-club to the creek, for example, reveals how short Egbo's
present is of the potential of his past. A similar use of *time* reveals
Sekoni. At his first appearance Sekoni contests Egbo's understanding of the past. Egbo demands to know why the dead should not be
forgotten if they 'are not strong enough to be ever-present in our
being' (p. 9). Sekoni, who has a terrible stutter, replies:

> 'Ththat is why wwe must acc-c-cept the universal d-d-dome, b-b-
> because ththere is no d-d-direction. The b-b-bridge is the d-d-dome
> of rreligion and b-b-bridges d-d-don't g-g-go from hhhere to
> ththere; a bridge also faces backwards.' (p. 9)

Sekoni's protest is for continuity. Where Egbo sees the past as
parasitic on the present, Sekoni sees it as unified with the present
and the future. The unifying force is faith. Sekoni's idealism is
ironised by his inability to speak it eloquently although his protest
finds lucid expression in his carving of 'The Wrestler', which depicts
the archetypal struggle to make sense of the world. This vision of
continuity was arrived at after an initial failure whose shock was

greater for the naive optimism which preceded it. The naivety is effectively figured in the self-importance of the inflated rhetoric of his reflections on board ship as he makes his way home (p. 26). Obi Okonkwo in *No Longer At Ease* (1960) returns with similar naivety and is forced into corruption; Sekoni is thwarted into a breakdown. Out of this crisis of conceptions of 'progress' comes his 'discovery' of continuity. The self-expression that comes about with this knowledge makes the carving an act of 'frenzy and desperation, as if time stood in his way' (p. 100).[3] Despite his new knowledge, though, he is killed because of his 'short-sightedness':

> The Dome cracked above Sekoni's short-sighted head one messy night. Too late he saw the insanity of a lorry parked right in his path, a swerve turned into a skid and cruel arabesques of tyres. A futile heap of metal, and Sekoni's body lay surprised across the open door, showers of laminated glass around him, his beard one fastness of blood and wet earth. (p. 155)

Characteristically, Egbo 'fled to the rocks by the bridge until the funeral was over where unseen he shed his bitter, angry tears' (p. 155). Sagoe, the cynical journalist, is 'locked in beer and vomit for a week'. Kola, the painter, worked 'blindly in spasms of grief and unbelieving', leaving to Bandele 'the agony of consoling Alhaji Sekoni', the grief-stricken father. Sekoni's death enables a comparison of Bandele's response to that of the others. In Part Two of the novel Bandele's gaze focuses critically on his friends. He probes their actions and motives, drawing attention to their inadequacy. It is no coincidence that Sekoni's carving of the archetypal struggle 'was unmistakably Bandele', and in Part Two we recognise the symbolic appropriateness of this.

Soyinka's novel, then, is not only an attack on the greed of corrupt authority, but also figures the intellectuals and the educated elite critically. Sagoe, for example, whose wit and satire is seen to full effect in the Oguazor party set-piece, is denied a more profound grasp of alternatives by the very destructiveness of his language. The incident sparkles with mockery of the hollow men of the new elite, and is powerfully recalled, though with a different outcome, in the chairman's party in *Season of Anomy* (p. 36). In the party at the chairman's house it is the military and the businessmen who are the point of attack, rather than 'bourgeois' intellectuals and corrupt businessmen. The depiction of Professor Oguazor and his wife, the tone of voice they are given to speak with, their absurd mimicry of European 'etiquette', identifies them as among 'the dead', whose brains are as 'petrified' as the fake fruit generously distributed around their house. A similarly bizarre image in *Season of Anomy* is the dedication of the fountain at the chairman's house: 'a Florentine moment in the heart of the festering continent' with a statue of St George as the hypocritical 'message' against corruption (p. 44). That scene, reflecting the altogether darker vision of the text, ends with the cloud-host depicting the slaughter of the innocents, a pre-figurement of the massacres to come later (p. 48), whereas in *The Interpreters*, the ends of the Oguazor scene are entirely satirical.

The satire is savage, but the effect is also to give us no possibility of perceiving what underlies their crassness. Sagoe wages the war against the Oguazors without a care, because he does not 'have to live with them' as the others do. He scourges them as scapegoats, but the symbolism of the act is diminished by his self-indulgence, which emphasises his contempt for social form rather than leading us to an understanding of their elitism. The uninhibited expression of his disgust, as well as his Book of Enlightenment – an academic treatise on shitting – establish his status as wit and iconoclast. He deflects scrutiny by references to this status. The Book is evidence of his predilection for the rebellious gesture, as is the eruption at the Oguazors' and the article on Sekoni which he knew would not be accepted. These gestures evade their complex consequences – that, for example, if he had to 'live with' the Oguazors he would not have made his extravagant protest – and shut off the possibility of alternatives.

If Sagoe is figured critically in his rebellions, Egbo is seen as a violent, obstinate man, both astonishingly daring and surprisingly uncertain and introspective. His obsession with the past is the means of measuring him against it, and finding him short of the early daring and curiosity. We can contrast this with the Egbo who had gone to spend the night by the water of the Oshun grove at

Oshogbo as a child, and who had found eventually a confinement in
the stillness and depth of the quiet water:

> I loved life to be still, mysterious. . . . But later, I began to go
> further, down towards the old suspension bridge where the water
> ran freely, over rocks and white sand. And there was sunshine.
> There was depth also in that turbulence. . . . It was so different
> from the grove where depth swamped me; at the bridge it was
> elusive, you had to pierce it, arrowed like a bird. (p. 9)

Egbo is seduced by both the quiet 'depth' of the grove, signifying
the silted calm of tradition, and the turbulence, and relative
freedom, of a changing world. Yet he sees the choices ahead of him
only as kinds of death, 'merely a question of drowning . . .
resolving itself always only into a choice of drowning' (p. 120). The
debate between dynamism and stagnation in the context of
'tradition' is taken beyond such ambivalence in *Season of Anomy*,
as we shall see later.

Despite Egbo's self-representation as an unnerved victim, he is
figured as a 'predator on nature'. His 'apostasy' both appears to
give up choice, and allows the fiction of an impending decision,
when in reality it releases his hedonism. His seduction of the
unnamed young student makes the point. He takes the girl to his
'shrine' under the bridge – it is to her that he speaks the passage
quoted above – probes and examines her for his own needs and
takes her with 'eager hands': 'The centre pure ran raw red blood,
spilling on the toe of the god' (p. 134). She is a virgin sacrifice in
Egbo's shrine. That the text employs tropes of blood and sexuality
in this alignment has implications on the valorisation of sacrifice, to
which we shall return later. The particular sub-plot of the student's
seduction and sacrifice is resolved unsubtly, but it makes the point
about Egbo's predatory nature. The girl becomes pregnant and has
to leave the university.

At the end of the novel, Simi re-approaches Egbo. Soyinka's
texts abound in images of powerful women figures like Simi whose
potency derives from their sexuality. Like Iriyise in *Season of
Anomy*, Simi is a whore who exults in her power over men; yet both
women are figured as pliant in the hands of their lovers. But Egbo

no longer feels the liberating ecstasy of self-abandonment in Simi's presence. He now watches her as 'she walked towards him, eyes ocean-clams with her peculiar sadness . . . like a choice of a man drowning he was saying . . . only like a choice of drowning' (p. 251). The threat which lies beneath this conception of sensuality is expressed in terms of envelopment and suffocation. The Indian woman Taiila in *Season of Anomy* is also given a powerful, controlling stillness and her eyes are 'ocean-bedded' offering as Simi's did 'a choice of drowning' (p. 93). As Simi approaches him Egbo sees in the calm depths of her eyes only the stillness that had threatened to 'swamp' him at the Oshun grove in Oshogbo.

As we have seen, the method of Part One is a dynamic, contrastive technique which enabled some understanding of the interpreters' unease in their community. In this sense, their disillusion and disgust with their time marks them out as caring and aware. However, we also understand their unease with themselves and with each other, and it is Bandele's role to focus our grasp of their misgivings. The mode of enquiry changes in Part Two and views the interpreters through a mythic perspective. For example, both Parts begin with a rainstorm, but the languages of the two storms describe the shift of focus. At the beginning of the novel the rain is evoked with lyrical realism, in Part Two it acquires a ritual dimension: 'The rains of May became in July slit arteries of the sacrificial bull' (p. 155). It is during these rains that Sekoni is killed, his blood flowing 'into currents eternally below earth'. As in Part One, all the friends except Sekoni are at the night-club in the first chapter of Part Two. Only now they are listless and miserable, in Kola's phrase, 'wet, bedraggled'. His image of their misery derives from his painting of the Yoruba Pantheon, and references to the painting increase dramatically now and the subject becomes crucial in the text.

Sekoni's death results in a change in Bandele because it forces on him questions of mortality and the gods. To Sekoni, death was part of the continuity of life, figured in the metaphor of an infinite humanity. After a pilgrimage to Makka, he went on to 'the ruins of Old Jerusalem' where he stood 'awed, so wholly awed' by his 'heritage' (p. 99). It was on his return from this pilgrimage that he frenziedly began his carving of 'The Wrestler'. Sekoni, however, had not been able to express coherently this intense conception of the human self as immortal. Ironically, it is his death which refocuses his intense insistence on connections, and makes Bandele, in particular, take an interest in the risen-from-death Lazarus. His interest in death is consistent with the mythic traces he acquires in Part Two. He becomes a 'death-still figure' (p. 156); he is 'a palace housepost carved of iron-wood'; he is 'like the staff of Ogboni, rigid in single casting' (p. 244). As he pronounces the curse on the Oguazor clique he is 'old and immutable as the royal mothers of Benin throne, old and cruel as the *ogboni* in conclave' (p. 251). Before the end, he 'sat like a timeless image brooding over lesser beings' (p. 244).

Lazarus first appeared in the text at the wheel of the cortege of a 'shameful' funeral procession which Sagoe witnessed. Later he rescues a young thief from the crowd. Lazarus tracks Sagoe down to the night-club and makes the claim that he had died and risen again. He wants Sagoe to write up his story. The coincidence of the albino's approach to them so soon after Sekoni's death gives their response credibility. Sagoe's appetite is whetted by the likelihood of Lazarus being another fake prophet to be exposed. Dehinwa is repelled by the albino's leathery complexion. Egbo, who throughout the novel is alternately attracted and repelled by knowledge of immaterial experience, stared at the albino 'with morbid intensity, seeking like the rest to extract from his face the essence of man's experience' (p. 161). Bandele questions Lazarus, asking what it felt like when he 'woke and began to bang the coffin'. Lazarus refuses to speak in the night-club, 'where life looks cheap' (p. 161). He invites them to attend a service in his church the following Sunday, where he would tell them the story of his death. The rebuke anticipates the more sustained criticism that the interpreters will be subjected to in this section.

Lazarus can be contrasted with Sekoni. Sekoni was brought to life by the discovery of the connection between human lives in which endeavour merged over time into a continuous activity of self-knowledge and self-expressions. Lazarus comes to life by the discovery of a force outside himself, and by this discovery feels himself closer to God. Lazarus' experience, like Sekoni's, is intensely felt, and Lazarus' gift is to be able to articulate it where

Sekoni stammered. Lazarus saw human potential for both evil and good, and after his three days with the dead he sees himself as the living link between the self's humanity and its divinity. He attempts to effect a transformation in the young thief he had rescued from the crowd, and whom he baptises Noah, as an offering to God 'because we fear that the Lord may have forgotten His covenant with earth' (p. 173). The friends are appalled at Noah's vacuity. Kola wants Noah for his Pantheon, to sit as Esumare, the intermediary between gods and earth-dwellers. In Noah's vacuity he sees the meaninglessness of the link between the human and the divine. He comes to see later that this cynicism limits his imaginative vision because it denies the human capacity for divine knowledge, and to deny this is to deny the dynamic relationship that Soyinka sees existing in Yoruba religion between gods and humans. For the gods return to earth not only to be present at their worship, but to renew the human side of their divinity. As Soyinka explains in his *Myth, Literature and the African World* (1976),[4] the gulf which appeared between human and divine impelled the gods to cross it:

> The journey and its direction are at the heart of . . . the relationship of the gods and man. Its direction and motivation are also an indication of the geocentric bias of the Yoruba, for it was the gods who needed to come to man, anguished by a continuing sense of incompleteness, needing to recover their long-lost essence of totality. (p. 27)

Or again, in the same discussion of the relationship of gods and humans, and of Ogun's role in facilitating it:

> Yet none of them, not even Ogun, was complete in himself. There had to be a journey across the void to drink at the fount of mortality though, some myths suggest, it was really to inspect humanity and see if the world peopled by the mortal shards from the common ancestor was indeed thriving. (p. 28)

It is Ogun who effects the passage through the 'primordial chaos' that separates man from the gods, and it is the rainbow, Esumare, that symbolises this joint of the earth and sky. To see Esumare as the mask of duplicity is to make a nonsense of the whole of Kola's Pantheon. Later, he analyses the artist's work as 'the will to transform' (p. 218). Kola's fear of 'self-fulfilment' as an artist is also a refusal to accept responsibility for the power to transform. It is out of this acknowledgement of his tentativeness that Kola can accept the divinity of the gods of his Pantheon, and conceive them as vital and alive. This is the meaning of the evocation of Yoruba mythology at the beginning of Chapter 16 (p. 224), and in Kola's recognition that Lazarus should model Esumare, the link between heaven and earth. Noah, as he explains, now becomes Atunda, 'the first apostate rolling the boulder down the back of the unsuspecting deity' (p. 224). The introduction of Lazarus in Part Two of the novel allowed the enquiry to shift from the inter-relationship of individual past and present to the potential for transformation that links the human self to its conception of divinity. The fulfilment of Lazarus' power contrasts with the tenativeness of the interpreters, whose cynicism is a form of justification for evasion. His failure with Noah, a failure he had expected to occur, demonstrates that the capacity for change lies within and can only reach fulfilment with the acknowledgement of the self.

The capacity for transformation, then, assumes that the nature of existence is contradictory. A clear example of this is in the way Joe Golder is figured in the text. Golder, who looks white but wants to be black, is neurotic with self-hate. Sagoe finds him 'distasteful', and that is before he discovers his homosexuality. Sagoe cannot accept the contradictions that Golder represents, contradictions which are such a crucial element in Yoruba myth. Obatala got drunk when in the middle of the task of creation and made 'cripples and the dumb, the dwarf, the epileptic' (p. 224). Ogun, 'the lover of gore, invincible in battle' who had with his own hands slaughtered his men and his children was also 'the explorer, path-finder, protector of the forge and the creative hands'. Sango, the god of thunder and the agent of justice, was a tyrant whose machinations and intrigues to pit two of his rivals against each other ended in his discredit, and he hanged himself before joining the other gods in heaven. Oduduwa, both a primordial divinity and a deified ancestor, is seen in some legends as a male god, co-sculptor with Obatala of the human form, in some other legends as the female arch-divinity, the wife of Obatala. A number of others are mentioned in the short passage at the beginning of Chapter 16 where Kola acknowledges the conception of Yoruba divinity as contradictory, and speaks of the co-existence of order and chaos, of the diviner god Orunmila and of the mischievous god Esu (p. 225). Most specifically, Golder models for Erinle in Kola's Pantheon, for Erinle is bisexual, a killer and a healer.

The contradictions are consistent with Soyinka's description of Yoruba myth having a 'geocentric bias'. The gods have great power and great compassion and yet are victims of their natures. In these respects, they possess qualities which humans share. Ogun's love of gore does not diminish his daring and his labours in hacking down the primordial forest by an act of will. If Ogun, the slaughterer of his own children, is capable of care and compassion, why should not Joe Golder dramatise the potential for resolving the con-tradictions in his nature? Egbo responds to Golder as to contagion. He first meets him in Kola's studio. Golder had sneaked in to look at the canvas, as had Egbo. Egbo is unhappy with the way that Ogun is depicted only as a blood-thirsty maniac: 'there is Ogun of the forge, Ogun as the primal artisan . . . but he leaves all that to record me as this bestial gore-blinded thug!' (p. 233). What Egbo complains of here is that Kola gives no indication of Ogun's contradictory nature, and it is significant that he is made to say this to Golder.

He discovers Golder's homosexuality on the night that Noah died. It is then that he finds out that Golder had taken Noah to his flat and frightened him by making homosexual advances to him. In his panic, Noah had fallen off the balcony and died. Golder is a nervous wreck in the back of the car, and Egbo is patting Golder's knee comfortingly as he makes this discovery. His reaction is described without ambiguity:

> As from vileness below human imagining Egbo snatched his hand away, his face distorted with revulsion and a sense of the degrading contamination. He threw himself forward, away even from the back seat, staring into the sagging figure at the back as at some noxious

insect, and he felt his entire body crawl in disgust. His hand which had touched Joe Golder suddenly felt foreign to his body and he got out of the car and wiped it on grass dew. Bandele and Kola stared at him, isolated from this hatred they had not known in Egbo, and the sudden angry spasms that seemed to overtake each motion of his body. (p. 237)

What Egbo had demanded of Kola's depiction of Ogun, that he should not have ignored the poetic possibilities of Ogun's contradictions, he is unable to achieve himself in his response to Joe Golder. In this instance, Egbo fails by any standards of human compassion, but he also fails because he is shown to be inadequate to the creative contradictions that characterise the gods.

As the novel draws to a conclusion, the criticism of Egbo mounts, and Bandele's status as the judge of his friend's actions gains emphasis. His criticism establishes the potential that Bandele sees in Egbo, and therefore implies the great waste that his failure to live to that potential is. Egbo rises to leave in anger, but Bandele is not finished yet. He passes him a message from the girl, the student that Egbo had made pregnant: 'When you are sure what you want to do you are to tell me and I will pass it on' (p. 242). Egbo complains: 'Bandele, Bandele, this torturer role does not become you,' but Bandele has become 'a palace housepost carved of iron-wood', and he is unbending: 'I wish to keep my involvement to the minimum. So please, only reply when you choose, nothing more' (p. 243). Bandele's stiffness with his friends does not derive only from the anger that he feels at their failures, but from the responsibility that he feels thrust upon him by those failures. He has to be 'like the staff of Ogboni, rigid in single casting' (p. 244), not because his friends have exasperated him beyond care, but because he attempts to force them to face their evasions. As he sat separate from them in the theatre: 'It was as if he had neither pity nor indulgence, and yet the opposite was true' (p. 244).

Egbo is drawn from his wanderings by the voice of Joe Golder singing 'Sometimes I Feel Like a Motherless Child', and as Golder sings his agony, Egbo's compassion reveals itself in the 'stream of consciousness' passage in which he begins to understand Golder's sense of exclusion and self-rejection. The method allows us a deep glimpse into the Egbo whose potential Bandele and Kola recognise and admire, the Egbo whose failure is greatest in the novel because his potential is so much greater.

Superficially, *The Interpreters* is a 'difficult' novel, but there is also a very clear structure, both in the sense of chapter construction and in the more dynamic sense of technique and method. In terms of chapter construction, the two parts of *The Interpreters* reflect each other.[5] In terms of method, we have remarked on the use of the past to probe the inadequacies of the present, and this is the most pronounced and a highly successful technique, especially in Part One. The subtlety of the symbolism, as is evident in other Soyinka texts which treat 'tradition', is that it recognises that the past has an ambivalent influence. While it illuminates the potential of the present, it also absorbs the energies of the present to resurrect itself. It is only thus that the past comes to have significance in the self-conception of the community. But unless the influence of the past is seen in dynamic equilibrium with the need for change in the present, it becomes merely a thing of 'death' rather than a revitalising force. Egbo is figured as understanding the dilemma but unable to accept the challenge. Soyinka uses the Yoruba religion as metaphor both to point to the human capacity for self-transformation, and to measure the interpreters against it, and demonstrate their weaknesses.

Season of Anomy, though constructed to a more compact mythic metaphor than *The Interpreters*, is both a less effective and a more problematic text. The central metaphor is based on the story of Orpheus and Eurydice, re-named closely enough as Ofeyi and Iriyise. The most basic version of the Orpheus story – there are many variations and an ancient religious cult arose out of the myth – has the hero descending into the Underworld to ask for the return of his lover Eurydice, who had been bitten by a snake and died. Orpheus, who is a poet and singer, wins over the guardians of the Underworld with his words (songs and poems) and Eurydice is released, on condition that he does not look back. He does, and therefore she dies again and is returned to the Underworld. Soyinka analogises this myth more or less precisely, except for one major change. Iriyise is rescued from the 'Underworld', without any conditions. Soyinka's text re-writes the tragic end of the Orpheus story, and in due course we shall see why it does this.

The real concern of the novel is to debate the choice of political action, and this choice is dramatised in Ofeyi's increasing radicalisation in the face of the Cartel's pitiless logic. The novel was published in 1973, after *Madmen and Specialists* (1971) and *The Man Died* (1972), all three after the Civil War and Soyinka's imprisonment, and all three centrally concerned with the events of these years. The Cartel is the combination of the three leaders of the pre-war Nigerian Federation (although Nigeria is not mentioned in the text), who come together to eliminate competition with cut-throat cynicism. Ofeyi works for the Cocoa Board, which markets the cocoa to the nation as a substitute for all the other things the people are denied. He writes advertising songs and produces fantastic promotions in which Iriyise stars as the luscious meat of the cocoa-pod. Unknown to the company, these songs and promotions are deliberately ambiguous and subversive. This is the level of Ofeyi's political action at the opening of the novel. A number of events take place which make it impossible to continue this low-key (and probably not uncomfortable) rebellion.

The promotions team visits Aiyéró, a commune which is self-sufficient, worldly-wise, tolerant and contemptuous of money – different in every respect from the Nigeria of the Cartel and therefore in opposition to its greedy ethos. Aiyéró at first recalls the incident of Egbo's ancestral village in *The Interpreters*. It is isolated and is figured as more continuous with its earth than the city. The elders of Aiyéró ask Ofeyi to become 'the Guardian of the Grain', a kind of first-among-equals in the hierarchy of the community, as the elders of Osa had asked Egbo to become their king. Ofeyi too refuses, feeling the 'stagnation which clings to places like this' (p. 6). But the more Ofeyi learns about Aiyéró, its rejection of Christianity in preference for an older and more rooted tradition, and its egalitarian and life-sustaining ethos, the more persuasive he finds the offer. After the failure of his subversive 'promotions', and a spell of 'study tour' abroad, he sees Aiyéró's offer as a means of another kind of political activism:

The goals were clear enough, the dream a new concept of labouring hands across artificial frontiers, the concrete, affective presence of Aiyéró throughout the land, undermining the Cartel's super-structure of robbery, indignities and murder, ending the new phase of slavery. (p. 27)

Aiyéró's humane philosophy and its willing adherents are to be both example and cadre of the new transformations. The project is later re-stated more prosaically as 'to create working-class kinships as opposed to the tribal' (p. 170). Aiyéró's rootedness in the land is symbolised by the pool at the heart of the settlement and by the rituals for the funeral of the Guardian of the Grain. The pool has an appearance of being a deep 'subterranean lake' silted with 'history' (p. 88), the atmosphere around it 'a dense-textured drape . . . sealing them within the dark preserve of spirits, placid and protective'. It is a place mysteriously sanctified against petty intrusion. In the past it had been a sanctuary from slave raiders who had the 'Cross-river whiff of violence, rape and death' (p. 89). In this pool-sanctuary Ofeyi receives the recognition of the spirits of the place, confirming his non-alienation, his rootedness:

He felt borne on a vintage fluid and potency of the past, as if invisible denizens of that space had lain their hands on him. (p. 90)

The image of history as the real transformed into the mythical is connected to Alonso's change into a figure of fantasy after his death in Ariel's Song in *The Tempest*. Soyinka's text makes this connec-tion concrete by quoting three fragments from the Song: 'full fathom five his father lies . . . of his bones are coral made . . . those are pearls . . .' (p. 90). So the 'undertows' of history, so dangerous in *The Interpreters*, are seen here as a force to be released, a coiled dynamism camouflaged by surface calm: 'This pond denied even its undertows, presenting a clean slate of perpetual calm' (p. 92). At the heart of Aiyéró, then, past human suffering and endeavour is transformed into a silt out of which new life forms.

The funeral rites for the Guardian equally celebrate new life. The

dirge brings the dead back among the living by locating their origin
and their return to the earth:

> A low moan rose, thrilled in the slumbersome air, the earth gave
> answer in trembling accents, a lead voice prompted the sleep-
> washed dirge of earth and a sudden motion of feet would thud in
> velvety union. (p. 12)

Then the dirge turns into a quasi-Dionysian dance with the women
stilt-dancers opening their legs to the humps of the bulls, celebrat-
ing procreation and death in the same ritual. The sacrifice of the
bulls, so dramatically evoked in the writing, is also figured as
renewal – willing beasts giving willingly to appease the spirits which
guard the ancestral world.[6] The lavish drama of its evocation, and
its valorisation of blood ritual as an expression of connectedness,
barely disguises what seems like a cruel pleasure in inflicting pain.
The sacrifice anticipates and is contrasted to the unwilling sacrifices
that are about to take place. For when Ofeyi's attempt at conver-
sion is engulfed in the larger terror of the Cartel's Cross-river
massacres, it becomes impossible to resist the Dentist's position
that the only way to fight terror is by terror. This is the climax of the
novel's argument, the acceptance that violence is appropriate
political action in circumstances such as those which prevailed in
Nigeria just before the Civil War. Ofeyi's position hardens from
acknowledging 'the claims of violence' to acting as if no other
action but violence is possible.

The crisis and its resolution between choices of action is brought
to a dramatic climax through the Orpheus metaphor. Iriyise is
captured and spirited away by the henchmen of Zaki Amuru, the
Cartel's strong-man in Cross-river. Ofeyi descends into this Underworld to rescue her, and in the process he is driven to the
unavoidable conclusion that only terror can succeed against a
terrorist authority. Before following this descent, we need to look
at Iriyise. Iriyise is figured as receptive to experience, so she takes
to Aiyéró 'as a new organism long in search of its true element'
(p. 3). If this appears a positive quality, a generous openness, it
also suggests emptiness. Iriyise does not know herself and 'seemed
to change under his [Ofeyi's] touch' (p. 3). Later we find her just as

receptive to 'the gin-and-tonic siren from the godless lights of the capital' (p. 7). This emptiness is also attested by the way she feels 'filled' by her initiation into Aiyéró, made complete (p. 7). She was a prostitute when Ofeyi found her and re-constructed her. As the Dentist remarks with grudging admiration, Ofeyi 'plucks symbols out of brothels' which when the moment arrives turn into 'super-mistress of universal insurgence' (p. 219). Iriyise was a prostitute whose ferocity and sensuality expressed her undirected rage until Ofeyi rescued her, and made her perform as the fecund earth itself:

> With Iriyise unbound, unearthed, salvaged, transformed and fresh-created, a grand design for the Cocoa campaign had crystallized in the flash of their first encounter, leapt from his hot brain entire. Goddess, Princess, Chrysalis of the Cocoa Grain, around her burgeoned a thousand schemes and devices, a panoply of adulation and Svengalian transformations, ending her immaturity and self-prostitution. (p. 94)

It is clear who runs this show. The image of fecundity is expressed clearly in the planting in Aiyéró – fecund earth and fecund Iriyise celebrated in prose of high optimism – and the meaning of her name as Dawn seems completely appropriate.

But Iriyise is also 'the bitch', and there are explicit references to her as the powerful female figure with potent sexuality who is also to be found in other Soyinka texts (Segi in *Kongi's Harvest* (1967), Madame Tortoise in *A Dance of the Forests* (1960), and, of course, Simi in *The Interpreters*). Iriyise is also 'Queen Bee', involuntarily at the heart of processes that she does not actively control: 'Iriyise occupied a cell in a deep hive . . . And Iriyise was Queen Bee of the hive' (p. 58). Finally, her 'moods' are unpredictable and therefore apparently out of her control (p. 81). It is clear that Iriyise is, in a profound sense, 'natural', an instinctual creature. And because her instincts are sound (they have their source in a regenerative impulse imaged as fecund earth and Dawn), she puts her trust in Ofeyi and is pliant in his hands. This relationship describes the hierarchical disposition in Soyinka's texts of the male artist figure and the potent women who are attracted to him. We find an explicit statement of this in *Season of Anomy* when Ofeyi reflects:

Vision is eternally of man's own creating. The woman's acceptance, her collaboration in man's vision of life results time and time again in just such periodic embodiments of earth and ideal. (p. 82)

Ofeyi identifies 'woman' as instinctual and fecund and reserves 'vision' and 'ideal' for himself. It is a thoroughly reactionary idea of both 'woman' and 'the artist'.

Ofeyi is forced to descend into the Underworld when he receives news of Iriyise's capture. The events fall into historical shape now. The coup has taken place and the killings in Cross-river are the massacres in the north in October '66 (pp. 87–8). Ofeyi and Zaccheus travel to Cross-river, and in a series of encounters, the horrors that are taking place there are dramatised: the killing on the road evoked with remarkable power; the lake filled with the dead; the train full of corpses which stops over a bridge to dump the dead; the burning of the church described with chilling detail. It is quickly established that the Dentist has undertaken a campaign of counter-terror, of selective assassination, and that his killings precipitate rebellion among oppressed people. The Dentist gloats about the assassinations 'which in turn appalled and uplifted him' (p. 113). His action releases the retribution of rural people, whose 'visceral bond' is still intact, in contrast to townspeople (pp. 116–17). Once again this valorises and idealises the rooted rural community, even if here in its capacity for righteous violence. Ofeyi's attempt to organise reform had only resulted in the carnage at the lake, the Dentist's campaign releases directed retribution. The argument is already turning towards violence as the inevitable response in these circumstances.

The inevitability of violence is also confirmed by the nature of the adversary. Cross-river is a grotesque dystopia. The landscape establishes this. Nature is perverted in the parched, diseased land which is 'infected' with violence. Ultimately Cross-river is described simply as 'the territory of hell' (p. 192). Zaki Amuri, the Cross-river strong-man, is a monster surrounded by languid, sprawled shapes among whom is 'a young boy' – to signify that Amuri is a sodomiser. It is an 'oriental' court, with the petulant boy, the eager and aggressive clerk, Salau spread-eagled in contrition, and the 'hooded' and evil Zaki. The *ranka dede* bestialises

Salau into a whining, cringing figure, and whereas rural people are valorised as 'rooted', in Cross-river the archetype is of the cringing cowardly peasant who turns to beggary. It has to be said that these are predictable tropes of the north of Nigeria, and African Islam, generated by 'orientalist' discourses of colonialism. It is made clear in this scene that the killings are to do with the expulsion of new ideas from Cross-river, ideas which challenge the corrupt feudal order. The killing of the man on the road figures the killers as sadistic and brutalised. As they perform horrific mutilations on their victim, their 'faces betrayed neither thought nor feeling' (p. 164). Both here and in the description of the massacre at the lake, the killings are figured as perverted sacrifice, an image raised again in the description of the 'Anubis-headed multitudes'. These killings are contrasted with 'Ahime's scalpel of light' which symbolised the regenerative nature of sacrifice.

Event after event intensifies the horror as Ofeyi and Zaccheus search for Iriyise. They descend into the morgue where the human body lies 'piece-meal', they visit the underground sanctuary in the church which is littered with bodies, and eventually Ofeyi enters the prison, in the innermost circle of which he finds Iriyise and where he is himself also imprisoned. It is significant that he converts the guard with words, but it is ultimately the intervention of the Dentist which releases Ofeyi and Iriyise from prison, the triumph of violence over violence. At the novel's end, the tragedy of Orpheus's glance back is replaced by the column of prisoners setting off on a long march as dawn rises.

The novel then, debates and resolves the issue of appropriate political action in an oppressive state: 'the claims of violence' are irresistible. The debate is effectively dramatised in the way we have discussed, but the analysis of the issue in the conversations between Ofeyi and the Dentist, and Ofeyi and the Indian doctor, lacks conviction. This is partly because the language in which it is offered is melodramatic and partly because the dilemma is posed in such a simple and unproblematised way (for example pp. 103–4). The portrayal of Cross-river as evil contagion – the massacres are 'bloodlust' which is 'a legacy of the climate' – simplifies the issue to an incredible extent. If the terrorist state is like Cross-river, the argument appears to go, then violence is justified.

Further simplification occurs in the opposition of the idealised campaign to transform the country through the humane philosophy of Aiyéró, and the violence of the Dentist. Such an opposition may make dramatic sense, but in a fictional text which insists on placing its mythic metaphors within a realist context, it is both unsubtle and manipulative. It makes the triumph of the Dentist's retributive righteousness all but inevitable. In contrast to *The Interpreters*, where a superb concert is achieved between method and substance, *Season of Anomy* valorises myth over the demands of language and voice. Political dispositions are presented without irony and are often overtaken by a tough-talking 'radical' voice, and the fiction of competing languages and metaphors in which *The Interpreters* is written deteriorates, at worst, to the cartoon language of student politics. Despite the great power of the set-piece scenes of the killings, *Season of Anomy* is undercut by the very passion which is at the heart of its argument.

1 Wole Soyinka, *The Interpreters*, London: André Deutsch, 1965. (Page references to the Heinemann edition, 1970, reprinted 1976.)

2 Wole Soyinka, *Season of Anomy*, London: Rex Collings Ltd, 1973. (Page reference to the Arena edition, 1988.)

3 It is not uncommon for the artist-figure to create in 'frenzy' in Soyinka's texts, or for the lesser artist to appear unable to achieve this state of release. A notable example of both is Demoke in *A Dance of the Forests* (1960), where at first the artist is afraid of heights and cannot carve, but his murder of Oremole releases him into a 'frenzy' of creativity:

> and I
> Demoke, sat in the shoulders of the tree,
> My spirit set free and singing, my hands,
> My father's hands possessed by demons of blood
> And I carved three days and nights till tools
> Were blunted, and these hands, my father's hands
> Swelled big as the tree-trunk

> *Collected Plays 1*, London: Oxford University Press, 1973, p. 27.

Equally, in *The Interpreters*, Kola speaks of himself applying the brakes to his talent when he should let go: 'At his elbow was the invisible brake which drew him back from final transportation in the act' (p. 218).

4 Wole Soyinka, *Myth, Literature and the African World*, Cambridge: Cambridge University Press, 1976, p. 27.

5 Part One begins at the night-club, takes us to eat with the Faseyis and introduces us to Simi as an image of female sensuality. This is followed by the long chapter which deals with the corruption of the big men. We see Sekoni and Kola at work. There is a funeral. We witness the chase of Noah. We see the 'sacrifice' of the girl at Egbo's 'shrine' and we attend the Oguazor party. Part Two also begins at the night-club. We meet Lazarus and hear his story, a contrast to the self-centred corruption of the old guard. We meet Joe Golder, an image of another kind of sensuality. We eat with the Faseyis again. We witness another chase, again involving Noah. There is a second funeral, this time of Sekoni. We see Kola at work on his canvas. There is another sacrifice, the death of the boy Noah, and the novel ends with a confrontation with the Oguazors once again.

6 This is how Soyinka puts it in *Myth, Literature and the African World*, p. 31: 'It is because of the reality of this [transitional] gulf, this abyss, so crucial to Yoruba cosmic ordering, that Ogun becomes a key figure in understanding the Yoruba metaphysical world. The gulf is what must constantly be diminished . . . by sacrifices, rituals, ceremonies of appeasement to the cosmic powers which lie guardian to the gulf.'

Wole Soyinka and the Àtuńdá Ideal: a Reading of Soyinka's Poetry

NIYI OSUNDARE

At the very core of Yoruba culture and philosophy is the Àtuńdá/ Àtǫǫ́dá paradigm.[1] In the beginning all power, all truth, all knowledge was vested in, symbolised, and personified by Òrìṣàńlá (the absolute godhead) who ruled the universe with unchallenge- able authority. Then, one day, as Òrìṣàńlá was resting at the foot of a hill, Àtuńdá, his slave, rolled down a boulder from the top, which shattered the complacent godhead into countless fragments. From each fragment arose a bewildering multiplicity of deities, authori- ties, truths, values, and consciousnesses, an eternal pantheon of paradigms and epistemes. But what ensued was multiplicity with- out chaos; the accidental fissures resolved themselves into a plural unity. A supra-segmental ontology was still in place delicate, intriguingly elastic. There was no civil war among the gods.

A fascinating mix of creative rebelliousness and rebellious creativeness, Òrìṣàńlá's epoch-making slave has his mission com- petently secreted in the morphology of his names:

(a) À	tuń	dá	(b) À	tǫǫ́	dá
Nominalising	re-	create	Something	from hand	create
element		make	Someone		make
		fashion			fashion

Implicit in both names is an essentially factive impulse; the verb *dá* common to both bears a deliberate, transitive import. But at work in (a) is a mytho-semantic game in which an abstract noun (àtuńdá), takes on a concrete (qua-human) accretion. In this collaboration of name-giving and myth-making, a significant

81

feature change[2] occurs: *àtuńdá* (re-creation), an act, becomes *Àtuńdá* (re-creator), an actor. The act does not only give its name to the actor; the process also becomes the person. Apparently helped by the passage of time, a mythic fusion occurs of act and actor, process and person, so that it becomes a literal, if not futile, exercise to differentiate the transitive verb from its equally transitive nominal derivative.

Àtoódá (something, someone created by/from hand) confronts us with a more intriguing morphology. *Oó* (hand) stands out here as both factive and metonymic. But the questions both myth and history have left unanswered are: whose hand? Could it be that of Òrìṣàńlá whose slave Àtoódá is? Are we then to believe that a moral lesson is being hinted here, that Òrìṣàńlá's epochal fate is his own making since he possesses a divine hubris which concentrates all powers in his hands? Is his fate, then, *àfọwófà* (invited by own hand; i.e. self-inflicted)? Or could the epithet be referring to the rapturous plurality resulting from the fragmentation of the god-head's hegemony – the lesson again that freedom, both human and divine, could, indeed, be 'something created by/from hand'? Like all mythic tropes and paradigms, the Àtuńdá/Àtoódá episode leaves us with a baffling open-endedness and mystic suggestiveness.

And a panoply of ambivalences. As is the case with most revolutionary initiatives, what is intended is oftentimes at odds with what is achieved; indeed, what turns out to be the consequence may be an ironic embarrassment to the spirit of the original cause. But there are also times when negative acts give birth to positive results: Judas's legendary betrayal and the Christian doctrine of human redemption; a destructive thunderstorm and flood on whose crest rode in Èjìbaùsì,[3] the wonder-child who grew to free his people; Àtuńdá's critical prank and the termination of an absolutist hegemony.

At work here is another reading more implicit in its triumphant humanisation of the godhead. Where is Òrìṣàńlá's all-knowing, all-doing power when, unbeknownst to him, the slave who bows to his every nod also turns out to be the author of his disintegration? Must a god also be the guinea pig of chronicling postmortems, having 'failed at divination' (*Idanre*, p. 78)?[4] So gods too have treacherous blind-spots in their eyes. So there are ambushes at the bend in the road beyond the limitless field of divine vision. The more human a god, the more divine; the more divine the more inevitably human. Even the supreme godhead, Òrìṣàńlá, operates in a political economy in which slavery is a source of labour. And we are not sure whether Àtúńdá's state of thraldom makes him a godlet in the service of a greater god, or whether that state 'rankshifts' him to the level of mere mortals. As Soyinka confirms in *Myth, Literature and the African World*, one of the most instructive characteristics of Yoruba, nay African, gods is their essential secularity, their almost tangible terrestriality. Between heaven and earth is that numinous bridge whose footprints point in both directions.

In psychoanalytical terms, Òrìṣàńlá and Àtúnda may be seen as two antagonistic elements inhabiting a corporate consciousness, one dominant and complacent, the other submissive but restive, one so sure of the eternity of privilege, the other acutely aware of his plight, and constantly, secretly seeking a way out – the case of a mind with two chambers, one frequently interrogating the other. In a way, every Òrìṣàńlá needs an Àtúńdá, or more appropriately, every Òrìṣàńlá creates his own Àtúńdá, the chink in an elaborate, overdetermined armour, facilitator of a revolution made inevitable by a crass, oblivious hegemony. Àtúńdá's boulder is not just a trope of vengeance (that would make it too personal); it is the symbol of a grand fulfilment, of a coming to pass. It is also another instance of a monumental happening initiated by a 'small' person, an individual action with prodigious universal consequences. When Prometheus stole fire from Olympus, he lit human way then and now, there (in Greece) and everywhere.

At this juncture, it may be asked: why this elaborate excursion into the Àtúńdá story, why this finicky exploration of its intricate morphology? Because in Soyinka, too, is the Àtúńdá ideal: creative and re-creative, iconoclastic, rebellious, libertarian and frequently revolutionary, an instant, almost natural, opposition to 'constituted authority', especially of the inhuman, totalitarian kind. A subversive, transgressive spirit in constant argument with customary 'givens'. Like Àtúńdá, Soyinka is a 'lone figure' (*Idanre*, p. 16), an icon of the individualist energy whose 'assertive act' (*Idanre*, p. 81) is capable of momentous consequences. Like Ògún, Soyinka's patron god, who 'sought retreat in heights' (*Idanre*, p. 71), Àtúńdá's judgement rolled down from the top of the hill. But beyond this spatial affinity, Àtuńdá and Òguń can confidently lay claim to other commonalities. Both are significant initiators of the 'awesome act of origin' (*Abibiman*, p. 10),[5] first in its evolutionary particularities and later in its revolutionary inevitability.

In both beings the act of creation is locked in dialectical combat with the act of destruction: Òguń is a warrior who slays blindly in war as well as a blacksmith who forges common ore into the miracle of steel, a hunter who dares distant jungles, farmer of dappled plenitude, drawer of blood and wine. A less titanic, though no less strategic force, than Òguń, Àtuńdá creates new orders by destroying the old Order, engineers a polyphony of accents from one invariate Voice. There is something Esuesque[6] in Àtuńdá's purposive mischief, though while Òrìṣàńlá's former slave is the unwilling author of a crossroads of dispersed consciousnesses, the Iron One is the proud owner of seven paths. There are so many other interfaces of morality and consciousness where both beings meet and mix. For in the last analysis, what is Òguń if not an Àtuńdá god, 'restorer of rights' (*Abibiman*, p. 23), rupturer of hegemonic silences?

A meeting point of myth, parable, allegory, and moral fable, the Àtuńdá paradigm contains the kind of transgeneric polyvalence which normally excites and exerts Soyinka's imagination. Indeed, in addition to an impassioned evocation of Òguń's lofty peregrinations, *Idanre* is also a triumphant celebration of Àtuńdá and the re-creator's ideal. In its sepulchral silence, Idanre rockhills themselves confront the Iron One with memories of the

> Union they had known until the Boulder
> Rolling down the Hill of the Beginning
> Shred the kernel to a million lights.
> A traitor's heart rejoiced, the god's own slave
> Dirt-covered from the deed . . . (p. 68)

with the crucial consequences that

> Man's passage, pre-ordained, self-ordered winds
> In reconstruction. (Piecemeal was *their* deft
> Re-birth) (*Idanre*, p. 69)

And in a deft stroke of intercultural, intertextual signification, Soyinka hurls the Àtúndá story across the abyss of time so that Àtúndá, Òrìṣàńlá's slave, roller of the Boulder of the Beginning, also turns out to be a primal scientist:

> . . . may we celebrate the stray electron, defiant
> Of patterns, celebrate the splitting of the gods
> Canonisation of the strong hand of a slave who set
> The rock in revolution . . . (*Idanre*, p. 82)

In this crossbreeding of myth and science, Àtúndá's 'splitting of gods' updates, by a stunning revolutionary fiat, into the splitting of the atom, acts which are both significant not only in the similarity of the violence of their means, but also the prodigious ambivalences of their ends. But Àtúndá could not have carried out this monumental act without Ṣàngó's fabricative fire, his 'stray electron' in the Iron One's ebullient forge. Ògún, guardian of 'the Creative Flint' (*Idanre*, p. 82), is thus part of the original separation and also one of the inheritors of its disparate cosmogony. Ògún's own Kiln also sunders into 'several kilns' (*Idanre*, p. 82), each soon to glory in its 'bronzed emergence' (ibid).

The celebration of the Àtúndá spirit is a celebration of difference, of a diaspora of values and visions, a diversity of talents and abilities. This is why Ògún, possessed by the Àtúndá spirit, is 'contemptuous of womb-yearnings' (ibid), undoubtedly an oblique reference to négritude and its desperate striving for uncritical homogeneity, its indulgent archaeology of a mythological African past. Let a thousand kilns glow, the Iron One appears to be saying, let each draw strength from its moulds of bronze. And in a bold transdenominational apostrophising, Àtúndá is showered with the author's baptismal accolade:

> All hail Saint Àtúndá, First revolutionary
> Grand iconoclast at genesis – and the rest in logic
> Zeus, Osiris, Jahweh, Christ in trifoliate
> Pact with creation, and the wisdom of Orunmila, Ifa
> Divining eyes . . . (*Idanre*, p. 83)

Prominent in this accolade is a conglomeration of gods from different places, across different times, empowered with different tongues, a theology of dispersals, of a sundered Whole seeking elusive unity in vagrant parts. A complex heterogeneity: dappled, varied, but also wild with disseminated terror. All a testimony to Àtundá's primordial daring.

A grand transformative impulse has always been close to the heart of Soyinka's project as a poet and person, a nagging, almost volcanic impatience with totalitarian godheads and their octopal structures; a near-Messianic passion to re-create, to re-make. Thus when, in the 60s, the boat of the fledgling Nigeria, overloaded with tribalism, corruption, and a reactionary leadership, was going down the sea of political turmoil, Soyinka was one of the first to point out the visionlessness of that dispensation and the tragic consequences that were likely to follow. When in the end matters came to a head and a civil war loomed menacingly on the horizon, Soyinka, again, was one of the few Nigerian intellectuals who warned against war and staked their lives in the pursuit of a just peace. The poet's 'continuing capacity to affect events in my country' (*The Man Died*, p. 12),[7] his natural repulsion by injustice, his patriotic search for a just, humane socio-political system in place of the neo-colonial contraption then in existence, provoked him to a risky, almost suicidal intervention in the Nigerian Civil War, an act which, in turn, led to his detention in solitary confinement by the military government of General Yakubu Gowon.

Soyinka's *Prison Notes* is clear on his mission and reasons for his arrest:

> . . . my denunciation of the war in the Nigerian papers; my visit to
> the East; my attempt to recruit the country's intellectuals within and
> outside the country for a pressure group which would work for a
> total ban on the supply of arms to all parts of Nigeria; creating a
> third force which would utilize the ensuing stalemate to repudiate
> and end both the secession of Biafra, and the genocide-consolidated

dictatorship of the Army which made both secession and war inevitable. (*The Man Died*, p. 19)

The above reads very much like a prose co-text of Soyinka's statement of intent in the second poem of *A Shuttle in the Crypt*:[8]

> In that year's crucible we sought
> To force impurities in nationweal
> Belly-up, heat-drawn by fires
> Of truth. In that year's crucible
> We sought to cleanse the faulted lodes
> To raise new dwellings pillared on crags
> Washed by mountain streams . . . (*Shuttle*, p. 6)

Energised by dynamic, action-oriented verbs ('sought', 'force', 'cleanse', 'raise', 'pillared', 'washed', etc), the early part of the poem ('Conversation at Night With a Cockroach') ripples with some of Soyinka's most patriotic, most romantic projects. But it winds down to a dreary dénouement as 'hate's dark waters' (p. 11) flooded the land, and 'The sky was blotted out in funeral pyres' (p. 10). The land was given over to 'death' and 'fear' and 'silence'. It is painfully significant that this poem's last line is 'As it was in the beginning', that gloomy refrain in *Madmen and Specialists*, another work of Soyinka's which sprang from the same compost of social history and personal experience as *The Man Died* and *A Shuttle in the Crypt*. Throughout, the poet moves between meditative hope and laboured despair. There is something elemental about Soyinka's address to the cockroach which reminds one of Lear's discourse on the heath.

Call *A Shuttle in the Crypt* a passionate diary of Àtuńdá's travails, the sojourn of a re-maker in the dungeon of un-makers, the plight of the dreamer in a bedlam of nightmares. Àtuńdá gets caught this time in the crucial moment before the rock's apocalyptic descent. For his daring he is thrown into the crypt where he lands not a lumpen bundle with its tongue in the sand, but a 'restless bolt of energy', a column of 'inner plinths' raised against 'unreason', against 'the dark-sprung moment of the trap' (*Shuttle*, p. 3). The 'shuttle' itself is protean: 'seed, shrine, kernel, phallus and well of creative mysteries' (*Shuttle*, p. vii), a fountain of 'inner repletion' against the barbarous aridity of studied mind-murder. Àtuńdá re-created himself even in gaol, building new ramparts, forging new channels of contact with a world from which he had been cruelly severed, establishing new relationships even within the circum-scribed commerce of prison, occasionally outsmarting the gaoler's iron edict with uncanny intelligence, and, above all, deepening his human impulses, plumbing those soft recesses where sympathy ferments and souls dialogue with the universe in a communion without words. They hurled Àtuńdá into the crypt like a trouble-some burden; Àtuńdá re-created into a thousand mysteries, Àjàn-tálá[9] which tames the terror of dark holes, the Iron One which may bend but never breaks . . .

The 'Four Archetypes' called up in *A Shuttle in the Crypt* all have the Àtuńdá trace. Take Joseph, the colourful dreamer, the straight one in a crooked world; pilloried for his dreams, sold into slavery, bouncing back eventually, triumphant. But Soyinka's are dreams which seek immediate and effective fulfilment: so much must have perished before the Seven Fat Years arrive. So, unlike the archetypal Joseph, Soyinka is no 'cursing martyr',

> No saint – are saints not moved beyond
> Event, their passive valour turned to time's
> Slow unfolding? (*Shuttle*, p. 21)

There is danger in delay, for

> A time of evil cries
> Renunciation of the saintly vision
> Summons instant hands of truth to tear
> All painted masks . . . (*Shuttle*, ibid)

Here, Mrs Potiphar, with the 'tattered pieces' of her 'masquerade/ Of virtue' and her 'painted masks', represents that apocryphal extreme, that bulwark of untruth which frustrates genuine truth. She is a disease crying for immediate cure by 'All whose dreams of fire resolve in light'.

Hamlet, 'the prince of doubts' (*Shuttle*, p. 22), has every cause –

personal and public – to live up to the Àtúńdá ideal, but he is disabled by a failure of will, withdrawing into graveyard musings and 'gallery of abstractions' (ibid). Unable to dare, too careful to venture, Hamlet becomes a trope for those trapped into inaction by fear of error. At a more immediate level he becomes a symbol for those dithering, prevaricating, procrastinating 'intellectuals' of the Ivory Tower (called 'charnel-house' in a later poem – *Shuttle*, p. 63), ever too ready to intellectualise and justify rank manifestations of the 'state's disease' (p. 22). These are the ghost-writers, special advisers, and hungry consultants to depraved governments, spongers on a nation's wealth – and will – more of madmen than specialists.

The Gulliver that is archetype here is anything but gullible. He is the principled artist in a state of Lilliputians, peacocks and sycophants, where

> The world was measured to a dwarf
> Sufficiency; the sun by state decree
> Was lowered to fit the sextant of their mind . . . (*Shuttle*, p. 24)

Where the Absolute Monarch, the 'Sun of suns', is 'Man-Mountain, King of Lilliput, Lord/And Terror of a thimble universe!' (ibid). In this funny and yet sombre satire, Soyinka injects a dose of Atundaesque irony: though recumbent, Gulliver is worlds taller than the standing Lilliputian 'giants'; their manikin realities run in inverse proportion to their gigantic illusions. In hard political terms, this poem is one of Soyinka's most caustic excoriations of contemporary tin-gods, especially of the African variety, those baffling throw-ups of history who scheme to reduce humanity to their puny stature, tyrants for whom 'foresight, insight/Second sight' are all but 'solecisms of seeing' (*Shuttle*, p. 26).

With 'Ulysses' the 'Haunting music of the mind' (*Shuttle*, p. 27) returns; landscapes merge with mindscapes. The transfiguring power of water arrives as a raindrop lengthens out to rivers. Water possesses a grand restorative, even curative, power here: 'We surf-wrestle to manure the land at ebb' (p. 28). The sea here is an ambulant, connecting force, epoch-maker, bearer of sublime footprints. While Gulliver's sea brings memories of a 'ship- (of state) wreck' (*Shuttle*, p. 23), Ulysses' tosses up images of 'quests', of storm-drenched energies straining at Fate. Here the lone wanderer, claim-layer to a 'heritage of thought' (p. 27), takes time out to interrogate the purpose of the quest, even the boon at its end: 'For how golden finally is the recovered fleece?' (p. 28).

A *Shuttle in the Crypt* is predominantly a psychological odyssey, the travails of the shuttle in the skull-ridden vault of thought-killers. It is thus a testimony to a personal anguish, the psychomental struggle against a vegetable existence. Even then, the collection leaves room for the airing of a few communal voices. In 'Ujamaa', dedicated to Julius Nyerere, one of the few, lamentably few, African leaders with the Àtúńdá spirit, Soyinka celebrates labour and its proletarian possibilities:

> Sweat is leaven for the earth
> Not driven homage to a fortressed god.
> Your black earth hands unchain
> Hope from death messengers . . . (*Shuttle*, p. 80)

before sweeping to an assertive peroration:

> Bread of the earth, by the earth
> For the earth. Earth is all people. (ibid)

And in 'Ever-Ready Bank Accounts' he wages a sarcastic, pun-powered war against Mammonism reminding us that:

> . . . arms
> Stacked too full of loaves cannot
> Embrace mankind. Ever-ready bank accounts
> Are never read where
> Children slay the cockroach for a meal
> Awaiting father-forager's return

In these last poems from Soyinka's second collection we can see the beginning of that deep-felt and clearly articulated concern for the poor and down-trodden which features so prominently in his later works. Mercurial, never slow to anger, Soyinka has the ears for the whimpers of those being pummelled by the muscles of power, and the grit and guts to rise in their defence. It is by no means an accident that the two poems constituting the Epilogue of this collection are dedicated to Victor Banjo and Christopher Okigbo, kindred spirits, both of whom fell, 'burnt offering' in the Nigerian Civil War, both of whom fought to restore our 'violated visions' (*Shuttle*, p. 89).

The more Soyinka got absorbed by African history, with its unending saga of humiliation, dispossession, and impoverishment, the wider the geography of commitment became. The more the poet watched the hopes and promises of independence flagrantly squandered by a treacherous African power elite and their foreign backers, the more vociferous, more articulate his voice of courageous dissent; the more desperate his search for a strategy of transformation. Apartheid South Africa constituted a negative epitome of the African's dehumanisation under an irrational racist system. The heat of liberation was on; *Ogun Abibiman* and *Mandela's Earth*[10] became Soyinka's poetical contributions to the struggle for 'race-retrieval'.

In building up the 'chimes of re-creation', (*Abibiman*, p. 4), Soyinka summoned Ògún and Shaka to the field of battle, evoking the two figures' legendary aversion to injustice, their readiness to fight for the righting of wrongs. The mytho-historical credentials of the two men proffer possibilities for collaboration: Ògún is the god of war and creativity, and, even more apt in the present circumstances, the 'Restorer of Rights' (*Abibiman*, p. 23); while Shaka King of the Ama Zulu is 'easily Africa's most renowned nation-builder. A military and socio-organizational genius' (ibid). When these two shake hands, when the forest joins forces with the Savannah, Africa will move 'From Slaughter Valley to The Hill of Destiny' (*Abibiman*, p. 12), a race of soldier ants will rid itself of the termite menace.

The swift materialisation of this 'savage truth' calls for a 'steel event' (*Abibiman*, p. 2), the abandonment of the grin for the *panga*, of 'Dialogue's illusion' (p. 5) for deliberate, decisive action. But it is all a strife for the repossession of 'stolen habitations' (p. 9), the restoration of denied rights, not an agendum for 'sightless violence' (p. 19) for

> Vengeance
> Is not the god we celebrate, nor hate,
> Nor blindness . . . (*Abibiman*, p. 20)

An urgency of vision, a nobility of purpose is thus the guiding
principle of the campaign. There is a constant need to

> Beware the life-usurpers masked in skins
> Flayed from the living forms of Ama Zulu
> Beware the jester masks with grinning teeth
> Of the corroded *panga*. (*Abibiman*, p. 17)

In that project of re-creation, that spirit of transformation being
urged, Soyinka bids us beware of re-fakers posing as re-makers,
present-day slaves and slave-makers who play at being Shaka while
constantly betraying Shaka's values and prolonging Africa's thraldom. As counter-figure and antidote to these parasitic usurpers,
Mandela looms large, an Àtúndá archetype, a 'black, unwilling
Christ' (*Mandela's Earth*, p. 1).

Soyinka finds Mandela's 'logic' both frightening and humbling: a
constant, solid spirit in an age that profits by shift, a captive who
'two decades' rust on hinge' (*Mandela*, p. 1) has left unbroken, a
prisoner who makes prisoners of his own gaolers. Mandela's
integrity takes Soyinka on an affirmative, though unsentimental
journey back to

> our indelible origin
> For indeed our pride once boasted empires
> Kings and nation builders. Seers. (*Mandela*, p. 15)

in a tone and tenor reminiscent of Ayi Kwei Armah in *Two
Thousand Seasons*. Mandela is the type who says 'No!' to 'seducers
of a moment's/Slack in thought' (p. 18), one who denounces
compromise and insists on justice, 'that rock/In the black hole of
the sky' (p. 20).

And he shares these attributes with many other figures in the
collection: Winnie Mandela whose bedspread the racist police

arrested, Ruth First, a white who sacrificed her life for black liberation, Dennis Brutus, 'Mr Boots, Knuckles and Bones' (p. 7), the heroes of Soweto, the trampled and dispossessed – 'shirtless/ Ghetto rats' (p. 16) of the cities who stake everything in the fight against Apartheid and its many evils. And just across the Atlantic, Muhammad Ali, another

> Warrior who said, 'I will not fight',
> And proved a prophet's call to arms against a war.
> (*Mandela*, p. 51)

By no means a blurry-eyed romantic, Soyinka is acutely aware of those anti-Àtúndá forces who stall the march towards regeneration and retrieval, the modern-day Matta Kharibus who hold Africa down for the foreign leash: Samuel Doe, Jean Bedel Bokassa, Marcias Nguema, Idi Amin Dada and the counterfeit Shaka presently slinking in royal shadows, soaking South Africa in reactionary terrorism. There is a constant need to look, think, and act beyond suchlike figures without failing to take their havoc into account in the first place. The tyrant may swing on the lamppost eventually, but *kílẹ̀ tó p'òṣìkà, nkan gaṅnaṅgaṅnaṅ ti bàjẹ́.*[11]

Soyinka is a poet of unlimited latitude, a free-ranging, though stubbornly rooted spirit for whom the entire world is a legitimate constituency. His fame stirs the lips of the Four Winds, but his charity always begins at home. Thus, when functionaries of the Shagari government unleashed on Nigeria's Second Republic a level of corruption and rapacity never witnessed in the country's history, Soyinka countered the rot with *Unlimited Liability Company*,[12] a work which shares the guerilla impulse and satiric ruthlessness of literary forebears such as *Before the Blackout*, *The Republicans*, and *The New Republicans* (dramatic sketches and skits which assailed similar evils during the ill-fated First Republic).

Unlimited Liability Company (*ULC*) provides Soyinka's most effective exploitation of the popular medium to date. Waxed on a long-playing record, simple in form and diction, it was on virtually every lip in Nigeria one week after its release in June 1983. The timing could not have been more appropriate, more dramatic: it came right in the midst of the 1983 electioneering campaign, and instantly established itself as one of the most vocal weapons against the corrupt incumbent government. A stupendous instance of 'song as dramatic performance' (Adelugba, p. 184),[13] its major *dramatis personae* were actors in the ruling party and its inept government.

Soyinka evokes the excoriative power of satire; and the satiric strategies for which he has become famous (or notorious: depending on what side of the power divide the observer is!) over the years come into full play: deliberate hyperbole, parody, burlesque, mock-heroic fantasy, *reductio ad absurdum*, piquant wit and humour. The barbs are primed at two major interconnected targets: government functionaries and stalwarts of the ruling party, and the Nigeria of their making. The former are so scandalously rich that

> Each time they sneeze millions of naira de scatter
> When they snore the bank itself go shake

and for them a private jet is a 'minor luxury': 'Mercedes na dash for their favourite singers'. When money for merriment runs out in the middle of the night, they throw open the bank for more cash. The 'Chairman' (or *share-man, sheer man, shear man,* or what have you – as in Soyinka's other works, punning is a weapon of verbal ridicule) is spineless, witless and near-moronic.

And, of course, his Unlimited Liability Company is Nigeria, a hapless entity already bankrupted by his 'Directors', the new self-styled warriors of 'Etike [Ethical] Revolution'. It is a country of hunger, disease, homelessness, a country whose 'national rubbish' is visible even to 'Russian astronauts flying in space', a land of anger. What Soyinka seeks to do is to deepen this anger, amplify it, then route it into the proper channels by laying bare the real situation for the people:

> You tief one kobo they put you for prison
> You tief ten million na patriotism
> Den go give you chieftaincy and national honour
> You tief even bigger dem go say na rumour

Monkey dey work, baboon de chop
Sweet pounded yam – some day e go stop.

The last two lines of the above excerpt are strikingly significant. Far
from being a threat or an angry boast, they represent Soyinka's
clearest and most unambiguous identification with the dispossessed
so far, and a measure of confidence in their ability to exact justice
eventually. Indeed, a lot of the import of *Unlimited Liability
Company* derives from the author's class distinctions: between
Country Hide who loots the nation, and Country Seek who are the
looted; between baboons who 'chop' and the monkeys who work.
There is no doubt that millions of Nigerian 'Country Seeks' who
sang along with Soyinka recognised themselves in his song. The
feast did 'stop' for the Share-man and his Directors when their
accursed government disappeared into History on the last day of
1983. Another board has since constituted itself. The 'liability' of
the 'company' still remains 'unlimited'. And so Àtuńdá's mission
continues . . .

It was Octavio Paz who said of Yeats: 'this poet . . . is several poets'
(p. 63).[14] No statement could be truer of Soyinka, a poet whose
voice began on a private, modernist note, somewhat art-for-art and
frustratingly obscure, becoming more and more public and socially
oriented as Africa's mounting problems made the writer's 'conso-
nance with the needs of the people' (Gordimer, p. 8)[15] an
inescapable necessity. We are inclined to compare the Soyinka who
monologued from the lofty heights of Idanre or the dreary darkness
of a lonely crypt, with the one who galvanised the marketplace with
the fluent, tendentious clarity of *Unlimited Liability Company* with
the principal aim of 'awakening a genuinely popular revolutionary
consciousness' (Izevbaye, p. 181).[16] We may sometimes disapprove
of his individualist, 'lone figure' approach to national issues,[17] but
no one can justly accuse him of silence – or inaction – in the face of
tyranny. In Soyinka we have a poet who, to borrow Seamus
Heaney's words, keeps 'telling his truth . . . with the authority of
experience' (p. xv).[18] Pioneer, pathfinder, bard of substantial

courage, this Àtúndá enriches our seasons with unending 'chimes of re-creation'.

1 For another application of the Àtúndá paradigm, see Biodun Jeyifo's engaging, unpublished essay, 'The Òrìṣàńlá–Àtúndá Dialectic: for John La Rose: Reflections on culture, community and diversity in post-Gorbachev era'.

2 I owe this term to Dr D. K. O. Owolabi of the Department of Linguistics and African Languages, University of Ibadan.

3 A legendary figure in Ikere folklore.

4 Wole Soyinka, *Idanre and Other Poems*, London: Methuen, 1967.

5 Wole Soyinka, *Ogun Abibiman*, London & Ibadan: Rex Collins in association with Opon Ifa, 1976.

6 Esu: Yoruba prince of pranks, king of the crossroads, god of mischief.

7 Wole Soyinka, *The Man Died: Prison Notes of Wole Soyinka*, Penguin, 1975.

8 Wole Soyinka, *A Shuttle in the Crypt*, London: Rex Collins/Eyre Methuen, 1972.

9 Àjàǹtálá: wonder child, mother's tormentor, precocious spirit – Yoruba belief.

10 Wole Soyinka, *Mandela's Earth and Other Poems*, Ibadan: Fountain Publications, 1989.

11 Before the Earth-god catches up with the evil-doer, a lot of havoc has been done.

12 Wole Soyinka, *Unlimited Liability Company*, EWP 001, Ewuro Productions, 1983.

13 D. Adelugba, 'Yapping – A Form of Patriotism', in D. Adelugba ed. *Before Our Very Eyes: Tribute to Wole Soyinka*, Ibadan: Spectrum Books, 1987.

14 O. Paz, *The Bow and the Lyre . . . The Poem. The Poetic Revelation. Poetry and History* . . . Austin: University of Texas Press, 1987.

15 N. Gordimer, 'Turning the Page: African Writers on the Threshold of the Twenty-first Century', *Daily Times* (Nigeria) (Review of ideas and the

arts), 20 February 1993, and 27 February 1993. (Reference in the present essay is to the 27 February instalment.)

16 D. Izevbaye, 'Assets and Liabilities: *Unlimited Liability Company* as an Artist's Investment in the Popular Cause', in D. Adelugba ed. *Before Our Very Eyes: Tribute to Wole Soyinka*, Ibadan: Spectrum Books, 1987.

17 Adewale Maja-Pearce has proffered a formidable argument in this regard: 'Always in Africa, it is the individual who must risk everything for an idea of what their societies could be, but this is inescapable in societies where the institutions of the modern democratic state are deliberately subverted by reactionaries . . .' *Who's Afraid of Wole Soyinka?: Essays on Censorship*, Oxford: Heinemann, 1991.

18 S. Heaney, *The Government of the Tongue: Selected Prose, 1978–1987*, New York: The Noonday Press, 1990.

Myth, Literature and the African World

KWAME ANTHONY APPIAH

I'm an Ibo writer, because this is my basic culture; Nigerian, African and a writer . . . no, black first then a writer. Each of these identities does call for a certain kind of commitment on my part. I must see what it is to be black – and this means being sufficiently intelligent to know how the world is moving and how the black people fare in the world. This is what it means to be black. Or an African – the same: what does Africa mean to the world? When you see an African what does it mean to a white man?

CHINUA ACHEBE[1]

Wole Soyinka writes in English. But this, like many obvious facts, is one whose obviousness may lead us to underrate its importance and its obscurities. For if it is obvious that Soyinka's language is English, it is a hard question whose English he writes. Amos Tutuola accustomed the western ear to 'Nigerian English'; Soyinka's English is only 'Nigerian' when he is listening to Nigerians, and then his ear is exact. But with the same precision he captures the language of the colonial, matter and manner: only someone who *listened* would have the British District Officer's wife say as her husband goes off to deal with 'the natives' in *Death and the King's Horseman*:

Be careful, Simon, I mean be clever.[2]

Yet the very same text recalls, on occasions, the English of Gilbert Murray's translations from the Greek – Soyinka, we remind ourselves, has translated (or, we had better say, transformed) *The Bacchae* – as here in the first recital of the play:

> Death came calling.
> Who does not know the rasp of reeds?
> A twilight whisper in the leaves before
> The great araba falls.[3]

The resonance is one among a multitude. In reading Soyinka we hear a voice that has ransacked the treasuries of English literary and vernacular diction with an eclecticism that dazzles without disconcerting, and has found a language that is indisputably his own. For – and this is what matters – however many resonances we hear, Soyinka writes in a way that no contemporary English or American writer could. It is important to understand why this is. For the answer lies at the root of Soyinka's intellectual and literary project.

Though he writes in a European language, Soyinka is not writing, cannot be writing, with the purposes of English writers of the present. And it is for this reason above all that Soyinka's language may mislead. It is exactly because they can have little difficulty in understanding what Soyinka says that Europeans and Americans must learn to be careful in attending to his purposes in saying it. For there is a profound difference between the projects of contemporary European and African writers: a difference I shall summarise, for the sake of a slogan, as the difference between the search for the self and the search for a culture.

The idea that modern European writers have been engaged in the search for the self is a critical commonplace. That it is a commonplace offers us no guarantee that it is true. But there is much to be said for the idea as it is expounded, for example, in Lionel Trilling's argument in his classic essay, *Sincerity and Authenticity*.

For Trilling, sincerity was no longer *the* problem for the European writer. Gone is the obsession with the attempt to bring what one is – one's self – and what one appears to be – one's role – into some kind of accommodation: Leavis with his 'engagingly archaic . . . seriousness'[4] is the last, late hero of sincerity, and the sin of sins

for him is hypocrisy. Enter authenticity, the paradoxically histrionic concern of existentialism and the beat-poets, which is also
central, to give a measure of its extent, to Proust and psychoanaly-
sis; the obsession with the transcendence of what one seems to be
by what one really is, beyond sincerity and hypocrisy. Authenticity
is an escape from what society, the school, the state, what *history*,
has tried to make of us; the authentic man is Nietzsche, his sin of
sins false-consciousness. In the world of authenticity, Freud stands
as a giant witness to the impossible pain of discovering one's inner,
deeper, more real – in sum – one's *authentic*, self.

> The artist – as he comes to be called – ceases to be the craftsman or
> the performer, dependent upon the approval of the audience. His
> reference is to himself only, or to some transcendent power which –
> or who – has decreed his enterprise and alone is worthy to judge it.[5]

The very fact that Trilling's language here will strike many
European and American literary critics as old fashioned is in itself
evidence about the character of intellectual life in the industrialised
world.[6] In the years since his death the language of criticism and of
critical theory has changed. But literary historians and historians of
ideas in the west are likely to agree that there is in their tradition a
sense of the writer as oppositional, whose roots can be traced back
at least to the Renaissance. Stephen Greenblatt has argued – in
Renaissance Self-fashioning – that Renaissance writers fashioned
'selves' from 'among possibilities whose range was strictly deli-
mited by the social and ideological system in force'[7] so that the
sense of a self fashioned *against* the culture is a fiction. Literary
history, by the very fact of attempting to give an account of the
writer in terms of a history within society, challenges the writer's
claim – which we find in Europe at least since romanticism – to be
simply oppositional. But it is exactly this pervasive sense of the
creative self as oppositional – so pervasive that Greenblatt's work is
interesting in part because it challenges it – that I take as given in
my contrast with contemporary African writers; and that sense is
not something Greenblatt's work undermines.[8]

We can find this conception articulated in Trilling's preface to
The Opposing Self, a collection of essays on various European

writers from Keats to Orwell. Trilling is discussing Matthew Arnold's oft-cited maxim that literature is a criticism of life. Arnold, Trilling argued, 'meant, in short, that poetry is a criticism of life in the same way that the Scholar Gipsy was a criticism of the life of an inspector of elementary schools'.

> The Scholar Gipsy *is* poetry – he *is* imagination, impulse and pleasure: he is what virtually every writer of the modern period conceives, the experience of art projected into the actuality and totality of life as the ideal form of the moral life. His existence is intended to disturb us and make us dissatisfied with our habitual life in culture . . .[9]

Trilling's particular concern with the transition from sincerity to authenticity as moralities of artist creation is part of a wider and distinctive pattern. Authenticity is but one of the ideas through which the idea of the artist as outsider has been articulated.

For Africa, by and large, this authenticity is a curiosity: though trained in Europe or in schools and universities dominated by European culture, the African writers' concern is not with the discovery of a self that is the object of an inner voyage of discovery. Their problem – though not, of course, their subject – is finding a public role, not a private self. If European intellectuals, though comfortable inside their culture and its traditions, have an image of themselves as outsiders, African intellectuals are uncomfortable outsiders, seeking to develop their cultures in directions that will give them a role.

For the relation of African writers to the African past is a web of delicate ambiguities. If they have learned neither to despise it nor to try to ignore it – and there are many witnesses to the difficulty of this decolonisation of the mind – they have still to learn how to assimilate and transcend it. They have grown up in families for which the past is, if not present, at least not far below the surface. That past and their people's myths of the past are not things they can ignore. When Ngũgĩ wa Thiong'o says that 'the novelist, at his best, must feel himself heir to a continuous tradition', he does not mean, as the westerner might suppose, a literary tradition: he means, as any African would know, 'the mainstream of his people's historical drama'.[10] It is this fundamentally social-historical perspective that makes the European problem of authenticity something distant and unengaging for most African writers.

We must not overstate the distance from London to Lagos: the concept of authenticity, though often dissociated from its roots in the relation of reader or writer to society, is one that can only be understood against the social background. It is the fact that we are social beings, after all, that raises the problem of authenticity. The problem of who I really am is raised by the facts of what I appear to be: and though it is essential to the mythology of authenticity that this fact should be obscured by its prophets, what I appear to be is fundamentally how I appear to others and only derivatively how I appear to myself. Robinson Crusoe before Friday could hardly have had the problem of sincerity; but we can reasonably doubt that he would have faced issues of authenticity either.

Yet, and here is the crux, for European writers these others who define the problem are 'my people', and they can feel that they know who these people are, what they are worth. For African writers the answer is not so easy. They are Asante, Yoruba, Kikuyu, but what does this now mean? They are Ghanaian, Nigerian, Kenyan, but does this yet mean anything? They are black, and what is the worth of the black person? They are bound, that is, to face the questions articulated in my epigraph by Achebe. So that though the European may feel that the problem of who he or she is can be a private problem, the African asks always not 'who am I?' but 'who are we?', and 'my' problem is not mine alone, but 'ours'.

This particular constellation of problems and projects is not often found outside Africa: a recent colonial history, a multiplicity of diverse sub-national indigenous traditions, a foreign language whose metropolitan culture has traditionally defined the 'natives' by their race as inferior, a literary culture still very much in the making. It is because they share this set of problems that it makes sense to speak of a Nigerian writer as an African writer, with the problems of an African writer: and it is because he has attempted with subtlety and intelligence to face some of these common problems that Soyinka deserves the attention of Africans.

*

I want to try to identify a problem in Soyinka's account of his cultural situation: a problem with the account he offers of what it is to be an African writer in our day, a problem that appears in the tension between what his plays show and what he says about them.

We could start in many places in his dramatic *oeuvre*; I have chosen *Death and the King's Horseman*. 'The play', Soyinka says,

> is based on events which took place in Oyo, ancient Yoruba city of Nigeria, in 1946. That year, the lives of Elesin [Olori Elesin], his son, and the Colonial District Officer intertwined with the disastrous results set out in the play.[11]

The first scene opens with a praise-singer and drummers pursuing Elesin Oba as he marches through the marketplace. We gradually discover that he is the 'King's Horseman' – whose pride and duty is to follow the dead king to ride with him to the 'abode of the gods'.[12] In the words of Joseph, the 'houseboy' of the British District Officer:

> It is native law and custom. The King die last month. Tonight is his burial. But before they can bury him, the Elesin must die so as to accompany him to heaven.[13]

When a colonial official intervenes to stop Elesin Oba's 'ritual suicide', his son, newly returned from England for the king's funeral, dies for him: and the Elesin responds by strangling himself in his cell with the chain with which the colonial police have bound his hands. The District Officer's intervention to save one life ends with the loss of two: and, as the people of Oyo believe, with a threat to the cosmic order.

The issue is complicated by the fact that Elesin Oba has chosen to marry on the eve of his death – so that, as he puts it:

> My vital flow, the last from this flesh is intermingled with the promise of future life.[14]

We are aware from the very first scene that this act raises doubts – expressed by Iyaloja, mother of the market – about the Elesin's preparedness for his task. When the Elesin fails, he himself addresses this issue, as he speaks to his young bride:

> First I blamed the white man, then I blamed my gods for deserting me. Now I feel I want to blame you for the mystery of the sapping of my will. But blame is a strange peace offering for a man to bring a world he has deeply wronged, and to its innocent dwellers. Oh little mother, I have taken countless women in my life, but you were more than a desire of the flesh. I needed you as the abyss across which my body must be drawn, I filled it with earth and dropped my seed in it at the moment of preparedness for my crossing . . . I confess to you, daughter, my weakness came not merely from the abomination of the white man who came violently into my fading presence, there was also a weight of longing on my earth-held limbs. I would have shaken it off, already my foot had begun to lift but then, the white ghost entered and all was defiled.[15]

There are so many possibilities for readings here: and the Elesin's uncertainties as to the meaning of his own failure leave us scope to wonder whether the intervention of the coloniser provides only a pretext. But what is Soyinka's own reading?

In his author's note to the play Soyinka writes:

> The bane of themes of this genre is that they are no sooner employed creatively than they acquire the facile tag of 'clash of cultures', a prejudicial label, which, quite apart from its frequent misapplication, presupposes a potential equality *in every given situation* of the alien culture and the indigenous, on the actual soil of the latter. (In the area of misapplication, the overseas prize for illiteracy and mental conditioning undoubtedly goes to the blurb-writer for the American edition of my novel *Season of Anomy* who unblushingly declares that this work portrays the 'clash between the old values and new ways, between Western methods and African traditions'!) . . . I find it necessary to caution the would-be producer of this play against a sadly familiar reductionist tendency, and to direct his vision instead to the far more difficult and risky task of eliciting the play's threnodic essence . . .

The Colonial Factor is an incident, a catalytic incident merely . . .
The confrontation in the play is largely metaphysical . . .

I find the tone of this passage strained, the claim disingenuous. We may, of course, make distinctions more carefully than blurb-writers and scribblers of facile tags: Soyinka feels that talk of the clash of cultures suggests that coloniser and colonised meet on culturally equal terms. We may reject the implication. There is, as Soyinka says, something so over-simple as to be thoroughly misleading in the claim that the novel is 'about', that it 'portrays', the relation between European methods and African traditions.

Still, it is absurd to deny that novel and play have something to say about that relationship. The 'Colonial Factor' is not a catalytic incident merely; it is a profound assault on the consciousness of the African intellectual, on the consciousness that guides this play. And it would be irresponsible, which Soyinka is not, to assert that novel and play do not imply a complex (and non-reductionist) set of attitudes to the problem. It is one thing to say (as I think correctly) that the drama in Oyo is driven ultimately by the logic of Yoruba cosmology, another to deny the existence of a dimension of power in which it is the colonial state that forms the action.

So that after all the distinctions have been drawn, we still need to ask why Soyinka feels the need to conceal his purposes. Is it perhaps because he has not resolved the tension between the desire which arises from his roots in the European tradition of authorship to see his literary work as, so to speak, authentic, 'metaphysical', and the desire which he must feel as an African in a once-colonised and merely notionally decolonised culture to face up to and reflect the problem at the level of ideology? Is it, to put it briskly, because Soyinka is torn between the demands of a private authenticity and a public commitment? Between individual self-discovery and what he elsewhere calls the 'social vision'?

It is this problem, central to Soyinka's situation as the archetypical African writer, that I wish to go on to discuss.

The 'social vision' is, of course, the theme of two of the lectures in Soyinka's *Myth, Literature and the African World*, and it was in this work that the tensions I have mentioned first caught my attention. Soyinka's essays are clearly not directed particularly to an African audience (hardly surprising when we remember that they are based on lectures given in England at Cambridge University). References to Peter Brook and Brecht, to Robbe-Grillet and Lorca, are intended to help locate the western reader. Indeed, the introduction of Lorca is glossed with the observation that it is 'for ease of reference'.[16] And it is clear from the way in which the first chapter (on Yoruba theology and its transformations in African and African-American drama) tells us much that it would be absurd to tell to any Yoruba, and a certain amount that it would be gratuitous to mention for almost any African readership.

Yet, it is intended (and to a large extent this intention is achieved) that *Myth, Literature and the African World* should be a work which, like Soyinka's plays (and unlike, say, Achebe's novels) takes its African – its Yoruba – background utterly for granted. Soyinka is not arguing that modern African writers should be free to draw on African, and, in his case, Yoruba, mythology; rather, he is simply showing us how this process can and does take place. He tells us in his preface, for example, that the literature of the 'secular social vision' reveals that the 'universal verities' of 'the new ideologue' can be 'elicited from the world-view and social structures of his own [African] people'.[17] I have every sympathy with the way Soyinka tries to take the fact of Africa for granted. But this taking-for-granted is doubly paradoxical.

First, his readership as the author of dramatic texts and as a theoretician – *unlike* the audience for his performances – is largely not African. *Myth, Literature and the African World* is largely to be read by people who see Soyinka as a guide into what remains for them from a literary point of view (and this is, of course, a reflection of political realities) the Dark Continent. How can we ask people who are not African, do not know Africa, to take us for granted? And, more importantly, why *should* we? (Observe how odd it would be to praise Norman Mailer – to take a name entirely at random – for taking America for granted.)

It is part of the curious situation of the African intellectual that taking one's culture for granted – as politics, as history, and, more abstractly yet, as mind – is, absurdly, something that does require an effort. So that, inevitably – and this is the second layer of paradox – what Soyinka does is to take Africa for granted in reaction to a series of self-misunderstandings in Africa that are a product of colonial history and the European imagination: and this despite Soyinka's knowledge that it is Europe's fictions of Africa that we need to forget. In escaping Europe's Africa, the one fiction that Soyinka as theorist cannot escape is that Africans can only take their cultural traditions for granted by an effort of mind.

Yet in Soyinka's plays Yoruba mythology and theology, Yoruba custom and tradition *are* taken for granted. They may be re-worked, as Shakespeare re-worked English or Wagner German traditions, but there is never any hesitation, when, as in *Death and the King's Horseman*, Soyinka draws confidently on the resources of his tradition. We outsiders need surely have no more difficulty in understanding Soyinka's dramas because they draw on Yoruba culture than we have in understanding Shakespeare because he speaks from within what used to be called the 'Elizabethan world-picture'; and Soyinka's dramas show that he knows this.

I think we should ask what leads Soyinka astray when it comes to his accounting for his cultural situation. And part of the answer must be that he is answering the wrong question. For what he needs to do is not to take an *African* world for granted, but to take for granted his own culture – to speak freely not as an African but as a Yoruba and a Nigerian. The right question, then, is not 'Why shouldn't Africa take its traditions for granted?' but 'Why shouldn't I take mine?' The reason that Africa cannot take an African cultural or political or intellectual life for granted is that there is no such thing: there are only so many traditions with their complex relationships – and, as often, their lack of any relationship – to each other.

For this reason, Soyinka's situation is even more complex than it is likely to appear to the westerner – or to the African enmeshed in unanimist mythologies. For even if his writing were addressed solely to other Africans, Soyinka could not presuppose a knowledge of Yoruba traditions: and these are precisely what we need to understand if we are to follow the arguments of his first lecture. Even when addressing other Africans, that is, he can only take for granted an interest in his situation, and a shared assumption that he has the right to speak from within a Yoruba cultural world. He cannot take for granted a common stock of cultural knowledge.

As I have argued in *In My Father's House*[18] it is simply a mistake to suppose that Africa's cultures are an open book to each other. That is one reason why the fact that I explain this or that Asante custom or belief does not by itself show that I am talking for the west. We cannot, therefore, infer a western audience for Soyinka's – brilliant and original – exposition of Yoruba cosmology. What shows that Soyinka's audience is western is the sorts of references he makes, the sorts of Yoruba customs he chooses to explain.

Now, of course, the only way that the misunderstandings I have been discussing can be overcome is by acknowledging and transcending them; nothing is to be achieved by ignoring them. And, despite the remarks in the preface I cited earlier, Soyinka knows this well. What I want to argue, however, is that the 'African World' that Soyinka counterposes as *his* fiction of Africa is one against which we should revolt – and that we should do so, to return to my earlier argument, because it presupposes a false account of the proper relationships between private 'metaphysical' authenticity and ideology; a false account of the relationships between literature, on the one hand, and the African world on the other.

We can approach Soyinka's presuppositions by asking ourselves a question: what has Yoruba cosmology, the preoccupation of the first lecture of *Myth, Literature and the African World*, to do with African literature? It is not enough to answer that Yoruba cosmology provides both the characters and the mythic resonances of some African drama – notably, of course, Soyinka's – as it does of some of the Afro-Caribbean and African-American drama that Soyinka himself discusses in *Myth, Literature and the African World*. For this is no answer for the Akan writer or reader who is more familiar with Ananse than Esu-Elegba as trickster, and who has no more obligations to Ogun than he does to Vishnu. 'Africa minus the Sahara North' – and this is an observation of Soyinka's – 'is still a very large continent, populated by myriad races and cultures.'[19]

It is natural, after reading the first lecture of *Myth, Literature and the African World*, to suppose that Soyinka's answer to our question must be this: 'Yoruba mythology is taken by way of example because, as a Yoruba, it happens to be what I know about.' In his interesting discussion of the differences (and similarities) between Greek myth and drama and Yoruba, for example, he says:

> that Greek religion shows persuasive parallels with, *to stick to our example*, the Yoruba, is by no means denied . . .[20]

as if the Yoruba case is discussed as an example of – what else? – the African case. Many other passages would support this interpretation.

Now if this is Soyinka's presupposition – and if it is not, it is certainly a presupposition of his text – then it is one that we must question. For, I would suggest, the assumption that this system of Yoruba ideas is – that it *could* be – typical, is too direct a reaction to the European conception of Africa as what Soyinka elsewhere nicely terms a 'metaphysical vacuum':[21] and the correct response to this absurdity is not to claim that what appears to Europe as a vacuum is in fact populated with certain typical metaphysical notions, of which Yoruba conceptions would be one particularisation, but rather to insist that it is richly populated with the diverse metaphysical thought-worlds of (in his own harmless hyperbole) 'myriad races and cultures'.

I do not want to represent Soyinka's apparent position as a kind of Yoruba imperialism of the thought-world. The motive is nobler, and I think it is this: Soyinka recognises that, despite the differences between the histories of British, French, and Portuguese ex-colonies, there is a deep and deeply self-conscious continuity between the problems and projects of decolonised Africans, a continuity which has, as he shows, literary manifestations; and he wants to give an account of that continuity that is both metaphysical and endogenous. The desire to give an account that is endogenous is, I think, primary. There is something disconcerting for a Pan-Africanist in the thesis (which I here state at its most extreme) that what Africans have in common is fundamentally that European racism failed to take them seriously, that European imperialism exploited them. Soyinka will not admit the presupposition of Achebe's question – 'When you see an African what does it mean to a white man?'; the presupposition that the African identity is – in part – the product of a European gaze.

I had better insist once more that I do not think that this *is* all that Africans have culturally in common. It is obvious that, like Europe before the Renaissance and much of the modern Third World, African cultures are formed in important ways by the fact that they had until recently no high technology and relatively low levels of literacy. And, despite the introduction of high technology and the rapid growth of literacy, these facts of the recent past are still reflected in the conceptions even of those of us who are more affected by economic development and cultural exposure to the west. But even if these economic and technical similarities were to be found only in Africa – and they aren't – they would not, even with the similarities in colonial history, justify the assumption of metaphysical or mythic unity, except on the most horrifyingly determinist assumptions.

In denying a metaphysical and mythic unity to African conceptions, then, I have *not* denied that 'African literature' is a useful category. I have insisted from the very beginning that the social-historical situation of African writers generates a common set of problems. But notice that it is precisely not a metaphysical consensus that creates this shared situation. It is inter alia the transition from traditional to modern loyalties; the experience of colonialism; the racial theories and prejudices of Europe, which provide both the language and the text of literary experience; the growth of both literacy and the modern economy. And it is, as I say, because these are changes which were to a large extent thrust upon African peoples by European imperialism, precisely because they are exogenous, that Soyinka, in my view, revolts against seeing them as the major determinants of the situation of the African writer.

Once he is committed to an endogenous account of this situation, what is left but unity in metaphysics? Shaka and Osei Tutu – founders, respectively, of the Zulu and the Asante nations – do not belong in the same narrative, they spoke different languages, their conceptions of kinship (to bow to an ethnographer's idol) were centrally patrilineal and matrilineal respectively. Soyinka could have given an account of what they had in common that was racial: but, as I have argued and Soyinka knows well, we have passed the time when black racism is possible as an intelligent reaction to white racism. So, as I say, we are left with common metaphysical conceptions.

Though I think that the appeal of the myth of Africa's metaphysical solidarity is largely due to Soyinka's wish for an endogenous account, there is, I suspect, another reason why he is tempted by this story. Soyinka, the man of European letters, is familiar with the literature of authenticity; and the account of it as an exploration of the metaphysics of the individual self; and he is tempted, by one of those rhetorical oppositions that appeal to abstract thinkers, to play against this theme an African exploration of the metaphysics of the community.

But in accepting such an account Soyinka is once more enmeshed in Europe's myth of Africa. Because he cannot see either Christianity or Islam as endogenous (even in their more syncretic forms) he is left to reflect on African traditional religions: and these have always seemed from Europe's point of view to be much of a muchness.

Some threads need tying together. I began this essay by asserting that the central project of that Pan-African literary culture to which Soyinka belongs could be characterised as the search for a culture – a search for the relation of the author to the social world. I then suggested that we could detect in a preface of Soyinka's a tension between a private 'metaphysical' account of his play *Death and the King's Horseman* and its obvious ideological implications. Soyinka, I went on to claim, rejects any obviously 'political' account of his literary work, because he wishes to show how an African writer can take Africa for granted in his work, drawing on 'the world view . . . of his own people', and because he wishes to represent what is *African* about his and other African writing as arising endogenously out of Africa's shared metaphysical resources. Most recently I have argued that we cannot accept a central presupposition of this view, namely the presupposition that there is, even at quite a high level of abstraction, *an* African world-view.

My argument will be complete when I have shown why Soyinka's view of African metaphysical solidarity is an answer to the search for a culture, and what, since we must reject his answer, should replace it. To this latter question, I shall offer the beginnings of an answer that is sketched out in *In My Father's House*.

African writers share, as I have said, both a social-historical situation and a social-historical perspective. One aspect of the situation is the growth both of literacy and of the availability of printing. This generates the now familiar problem of the transition from fundamentally oral to literary cultures: and in doing so it gives rise to that peculiar privacy which is associated with the written text, a privacy associated with a new kind of property in texts, a new kind of authorial authority, a new kind of creative *persona*. It is easy to see now that, in generating the category of the individual in the new world of the public – *published* – text, in creating the private 'metaphysical' interiority of the author, this social-historical situation tears the writer out of his social-historical perspective; the authorial 'I' struggles to displace the 'we' of the oral narration. ·

This struggle is as central to Soyinka's situation as it is to that of African writers generally. At the same time, and again typically, Soyinka, the individual, a Nigerian outside the traditional, more certain world of his Yoruba ancestors, struggles with the Soyinka who experiences the loss of that world, of these gods of whom he speaks with such love and longing in the first lecture. Once again the 'I' seeks to escape the persistent and engulfing 'we'.

And with this dialectic of self-as-whole and self-as-part, we reach the core: for this struggle is, I suggest, the source of the tension in his author's note – the tension between Soyinka's account of his drama and the drama itself. But it is also at the root of the project of *Myth, Literature and the African World*.

For Soyinka's search for a culture has led him, as the title of the book indicates, away from the possibility of a Yoruba or a Nigerian 'we' to an African, a continental community. His solution to the problem of what it is that individuates African culture (which he senses as a problem because he realises that Africans have so much in common) is that African literature is united in its drawing on the resources of an African conception of community growing out of an African metaphysics. The tension in *Myth, Literature and the African World* is between this thesis and the Soyinka of the dramas, implicit in his account of Yoruba cosmology in the first lecture, the Soyinka whose account of Yoruba cosmology is precisely not the Yoruba account; who has taken sometimes Yoruba mythology, but sometimes the world of a long-dead Greek, and demythologised them to his own purposes, making of them something new, more 'metaphysical', and, above all, more private and individual.

Once we see that Soyinka's account of his literary project is in tension with his literary *corpus* we can see why he has to conceal, as I have suggested he does, the ideological role that he sees for the writer. If African writers were to play their social role in creating a new African literature of the 'secular social vision' drawing on an African metaphysics, then the colonial experience *would* be a 'catalytic incident merely' – it could only be the impetus to uncover this metaphysical solidarity. Furthermore, his own work, viewed as an examination of the 'abyss of transition', serves its ideological purpose just by a *metaphysical* examination, and loses this point when it is reduced to an account of the colonial experience. Paradoxically, its political purpose – in the creation of an African literary culture, the declaration of independence of the African mind – is served only by concealing its political interpretation.

We cannot, then, accept Soyinka's understanding of the purposes of Africa's literatures today. And yet his *oeuvre* embodies, perhaps more than any other body of modern African writing, the challenge of a new mode of individuality in African intellectual life. In taking up so passionately the heritage of the printed word, he has entered inevitably into the new kind of literary self that comes with print, a self that is the product, surely, of changes in social life as well as in the technology of the word. This novel self is more individualist and atomic than the self of precapitalist societies, it is a creature of modern economic relations. I do not know that this new conception of the self was inevitable, but it is no longer something that we in Africa could escape even if we wanted to. And if we cannot escape it, let us celebrate it – there is surely a Yoruba proverb with this moral? – and celebrate it in the work of Wole Soyinka, who has provided in his plays a literary experience whose individuality is an endless source of insight and pleasure.[22]

1 Chinua Achebe, Interview with Anthony Appiah, D. A. N. Jones and John Ryle. *Times Literary Supplement*, February 1982.

2 Wole Soyinka, *Death and the King's Horseman*, London: Methuen, 1975, p. 49.

3 Soyinka, *Death and the King's Horseman*, p. 11.

4 Lionel Trilling, *Sincerity and Authenticity*, Cambridge, Massachusetts: Harvard University Press, 1971, p. 6.

5 Trilling, *Sincerity and Authenticity*, p. 97.

6 I have taken up this issue – which is connected, I think, with the increasing commodification of intellectual and 'artistic' production in what is called 'postmodern' culture – in 'Is the "Post" in "Postcolonial" the "Post" in "Postmodern"?', *Critical Inquiry 17* (Winter, 1991), pp. 336–57.

7 Stephen Greenblatt, *Renaissance Self-fashioning: from More to Shakespeare*, Chicago: Chicago University Press, 1980, p. 256.

8 I have tried to say more about the issues of agency that Greenblatt's work raises in 'Tolerable Falsehoods: Agency and the Interests of Theory', in *Consequences of Theory*, Barbara Johnson and Jonathan Arac (eds.), Baltimore: Johns Hopkins University Press, 1991, pp. 63–90.

9 Lionel Trilling, *The Opposing Self: Nine Essays in Criticism*, New York: Viking Press, 1955, pp. xii-xiv.

10 Ngũgĩ wa Thiong'o, *Homecoming*, New York: Lawrence Hill and Company, 1972, p. 39.

11 Soyinka, *Death and the King's Horseman*, Author's Note.

12 Soyinka, *Death and the King's Horseman*, p. 62.

13 Soyinka, *Death and the King's Horseman*, p. 26.

14 Soyinka, *Death and the King's Horseman*, p. 40.

15 Soyinka, *Death and the King's Horseman*, p. 65.

16 Wole Soyinka, *Myth, Literature and the African World*, Cambridge: Cambridge University Press, 1976, p. 50.

17 Soyinka, *Myth, Literature and the African World*, p. xii.

18 Kwame A. Appiah, *In My Father's House*, London: Methuen, 1992.

19 Soyinka, *Myth, Literature and the African World*, p. 97.

20 Soyinka, *Myth, Literature and the African World*, p. 14. (Italics mine.)

21 Soyinka, *Myth, Literature and the African World*, p. 57.

22 My discussion of *Death and the King's Horseman* is much influenced by Soyinka's production at Lincoln Center in early 1987.

Madmen and Specialists – New Nation States and the Importance of a Tragic Art

GABRIEL GBADAMOSI

As I entered I saw a young albino boy. To be a starving Biafran orphan was to be in a most pitiable situation, but to be a starving albino Biafran was to be in a position beyond description. Dying of starvation, he was still among his peers an object of ostracism, ridicule and insult. I saw this boy looking at me. He was like a living skeleton. There was a skeletal kind of whiteness about him. He moved nearer and nearer to me . . . It was beyond war, it was beyond journalism, it was beyond photography, but not beyond politics. This unspeakable suffering was not the result of one of Africa's natural disasters. Here was not nature's pruning fork at work but the outcome of men's evil desires. If I could, I would take this day out of my life, demolish the memory of it. But like memories of those haunting pictures of the Nazi death camps, we cannot, must not be allowed to forget the appalling things we are all capable of doing to our fellow human beings. The photograph I took of that little albino boy must remain engraved on the minds of all who see it . . . I wanted to break the hearts and spirits of secure people.

DON MCCULLIN, 'Children of Biafra'[1]

SI BERO: Not you yourself Bero, but guilt contaminates.

WOLE SOYINKA, *Madmen and Specialists*[2]

The Nigerian Civil War began with Biafra's declaration of secession from the Nigerian Federation on 30 May 1967, and continued with fierce fighting until the surrender of Biafra on 15 January 1970. Following several waves of pogroms against the Ibo people from the east of Nigeria living in the north, the mainly Ibo state of Biafra came into being in a climate of fear – fear of genocide. One lasting image of that internecine conflict, picked up by Don McCullin, is the effect of the so-called 'hunger war': the sight of the starving children of Biafra.

Wole Soyinka, a Yoruba from the western region of Nigeria, spent the years from 1967 to 1969 in prison for opposition to that war. A first version of his play, *Madmen and Specialists*, was produced abroad in 1970, in the immediate aftermath of the war, and the first complete version was performed in Nigeria in March of the following year. It deals with the climate of fear surrounding the war, and the apprehension of terrible things done.

In the play, Si Bero, a rather brittle figure of domestic virtue and integrity, waits and prepares at home for the return from the warfront of her brother, Dr Bero, and their father, the Old Man. A ready abuse of any obstacle to honest work is second nature to her. She is strong-headed. Nothing, it seems, can move, much less break, her heart; certainly not the four beggars going through their 'performance' – crippled, blind, spineless and in spasm – as maimed victims of the war:

> (*Si Bero approaches . . . The Mendicants begin their performance as soon as they sense her approach. Blindman is alms collector, Goyi repeats a single acrobatic trick, Aafaa is the 'dancer'. Blindman shakes the rattles while the Cripple drums with his crutches and is lead singer.*)
>
> SI BERO: (*As Aafaa moves to intercept her*) Don't try that nonsense with me. I live in this neighbourhood, remember?
>
> (p. 218)

Si Bero is a secure person.

Given that the direct assault of such a 'performance' on the sensibility of a secure person is seen not to be effective, it is interesting to see how Soyinka structures *his* play. Ostensibly, *Madmen and Specialists* is a classical tragedy in the western tradition. It observes the unities of time, place and action – with some adjustment for later techniques of freeze-frame stops in the action and abrupt lighting changes. One effect of this classicism is to keep a certain kind of propriety in the drama, known in the French classical theatre as *'bienséance'*, whereby the more gory details are narrated and kept off-stage. This would seem rather an austerely formal approach to so immediate a subject as the recent war. Particularly from Soyinka, whose grounding in Theatre of the Absurd and experiments with modernism and Yoruba aesthetics in earlier plays such as *The Road*[3] would lead us to expect a less restrained treatment of his subject matter. However, the tragedy of *Madmen and Specialists* is kept very much in the family of Si Bero and her menfolk on their return from the war.

Even the classical chorus is retained – the group of all-dancing, all-singing, maimed and crippled Mendicants. Yet it is with this war-like chorus that we have the first inkling of the mischievous, bleakly sardonic dramaturgy of Soyinka at work. The Mendicants, recruited by Dr Bero to spy on Si Bero and his own house (the classical *skene*, which in this play includes a prison-surgery in the cellar), want to do more than simply comment on the action – they want their own part of it: 'CRIPPLE: (*whining*) . . . We do nothing really bad, just one or two things to eke out the droppings of charity' (p. 232). Each member of the four-man chorus is strongly characterised, not least by their individual affliction. Moreover, they lack the discretion of either spy or chorus; like Aafaa, the ex-chaplain suffering from St Vitus spasms, they allow certain gory details about the war and their own function to leak out. They are always darkly hinting:

> AAFAA: (*posing*) In a way you may call us vultures. We clean up the mess made by others. The populace should be grateful for our presence. (*He turns slowly round.*) If there is anyone here who does not approve us, just say so and we quit. (*His hand makes the motion of half-drawing out a gun.*) I mean, we are not here because we like it. We stay at immense sacrifice to ourselves . . . They insist we stay.
> (pp. 220–21)

Not only the other characters on stage but also the audience are subjected to the peculiar menace of this chorus. St Vitus's Dance is a name for chorea, 'a convulsive disorder, characterised by irregular involuntary contractions of the muscles' (OED). It breaks every rule of propriety ever to pull a gun on an audience, let alone when the finger on that trigger is liable to contract involuntarily. The term St Vitus's Dance originated in a seventeenth-century practice in Germany – participants danced themselves into a state resembling chorea before a statue of the saint in order to secure good health for the year. There *is* something unhealthy about these self-proclaimed vultures, implying some kind of carrion under the floorboards of the house needing to be purged.

Above all, it is the robust physicality of these war-wounded, in their mutilated fleshliness, which starts to grate on the sensibility of Si Bero. They are in and of themselves gory, leaving the classical proprieties of '*bienséance*' in tatters. They themselves constitute the gory detail of the war refusing to be kept off-stage:

> SI BERO: Stop that noise! Did I ask you here for entertainment?
> CRIPPLE: No offence, Si Bero, no offence. We only thought you had forgotten us.
> SI BERO: And thought your horrible voices the best way of reminding me.
>
> (p. 226)

More than a chorus, they are unappeased and clamouring furies. The war, and the results of the war, have begun to arrive on Si Bero's doorstep, joining in and distorting her singing and dancing with their 'raucous, cynical tone' (p. 226). Here again is Soyinka's alarming dramaturgy. The dances of the Mendicants are distortions and transformations of Yoruba dance idioms into a compelling dance of death. Their 'performance' deforms the dance of Si Bero with Iya Agba, one of the two Old Women who are guarantors of Si Bero's integrity within Yoruba culture. It reminds her not only of the forgotten of the war, but of how deeply the Mendicants threaten her secure identity through, precisely, bringing into question the integrity of her culture. Si Bero has every reason to ask them to 'keep your voices down and stop frightening the neighbourhood' (p. 227).

The final voice raised on this miasma of contaminating knowledge is that of Si Bero's own brother, Dr Bero. On his return, his answers to her questions about himself, their father and the war are vague and evasive. Then, again, dark hints begin to leak into his

replies: 'We've wetted your good earth with something more
potent [than palm wine]' (p. 234). Si Bero refuses to believe that
either Bero, a doctor, or the Old Man could have become involved
directly in war atrocities. Nevertheless, she *has* known something:
'We heard terrible things. So much evil' (p. 236). Hers has been a
tacit complicity of knowing, and refusal to acknowledge how
closely the horror of war has come into her life. Her security begins
to resemble a fortress under siege. The war has come home, and is
inside the house, in the form of Bero and the Old Man. No longer
sure of them, she can no longer be sure of herself. Bero and the Old
Man have experimented with cannibalism, and taught it to the
Mendicants along with the rapaciously violent ethos of 'As', begun
as a grace over the eating of human flesh: 'As Was the Beginning,
As is, Now, As Ever shall be . . .' (p. 241).

> BERO: Out of your world, little sister, out of your little world. Stay in
> it and do only what I tell you. That way you'll be safe.
>
> (p. 241)

But Si Bero is not safe. She can no longer seek the security of the
house and her own place within it, any more than she can be sure of
what her brother, Dr Bero, the specialist, is capable of:

> BERO: . . . The Specialist they called me, and a specialist is – well – a
> specialist. You analyse, you diagnose, you – (*He aims an imaginary
> gun*) – prescribe.
> SI BERO: (*more to herself*) You should have told me . . . I swore I was
> sure of you.
>
> (p. 237)

Si Bero's silent complicity in the tragedy of the war is no longer
tenable. The tragedy is now in her own life: her identification with
Bero is faced with the impossibility of accepting his inhuman ethos
of power released from any moral compunction.

When I first read *Madmen and Specialists*, I recognised something
familiar in the predicament of Si Bero. It was the feeling of not really
knowing what went on in the Biafran War. My father, a Nigerian,
was in London for the duration of the war and to me it seemed very

far away. I remember having a short conversation with him about the play years after the war itself was over. Now, that conversation seems to be a missing piece in the jigsaw of my understanding:

'I'm reading Soyinka's *Madmen and Specialists*.'
'Who? The journalist?'
'A writer. It's a play about the Biafran War.'
'What do you know? It's not a joke. Don't believe everything you read.'

At the time, I couldn't understand why my father had Soyinka down as a journalist. He knew exactly who Soyinka was; they had met. He also knew that I intended to become a writer, so it was a mystery to me why he didn't have that profession marked down for Soyinka. Only later I realised that in Nigeria the boundaries between writer as artist, journalist and politician shift. Whereas theatre might be regarded as trivial, a joke, there were certain conditions under which the writer became war reporter. This dynamic engagement with Nigerian society explains some of the complexity of Soyinka's ironic positions. In his 1967 lecture, 'The Writer in a Modern African State', Soyinka observed that 'Poets have lately taken to gun-running and writers are heard of holding up radio stations',[4] ironising a 1965 incident in which he was accused of exactly that in protesting corrupt elections in Nigeria's Western Region. Cryptic, laced with irony as it is – and in despite of my father's wariness – I now feel Soyinka's play comes close to anatomising a reticence in Nigeria to do with plain-speaking.

But the question remains: what, after all, did I know? I have very clearly the memory of watching news reports of the war on British television. I didn't know then what to make of a dusty tank clanking along a road, or my father's silence. But that remains my image of the war, together with the news that the children of Biafra were starving.

What was re-awoken in me by reading Soyinka's play, was a need to locate the meaning of that war for my father, to retrieve, from an anguished silence, something of what he thought or felt – to know for myself by identifying with *him*. In attempting this, my own identity as an Irish-Nigerian brought up in Britain led me to identify

in ways I find hard to describe with the predicament of that albino
boy in Don McCullin's account of Biafran children at the start of
this essay. Ostracised and starving, the boy was looking at McCullin, presumably, because he was a white man. McCullin's eye was
drawn to the boy through his skeletal whiteness. These distorted
images of ourselves are capable of touching horror and compassion, but they also reach very deeply into our sense who we are –
they touch our identity. There is a feeling, as the boy edges closer to
him, of something like shock or panic. What McCullin realises, I
think, is that *they identify with each other*. To be able to see
ourselves in others, seems to me to be central in this way to any
tragic art – moments of recognition, like memory, never to be
demolished. When I think of myself as a Nigerian, I remember the
Nigerian rat-catcher who came to my flat in London for the local
council: 'Yes, you've got a rat. Sign here.' I signed my name.

> 'Gbadamosi?!'
> 'Yes.'
> 'You are a Nigerian?'
> 'Yes.'
> (*tilting his head*) '—I don't think so.'

When, despite the rat-catcher, I think of my father as a Nigerian, I
remember the calendars we had at home with pictures of General
Gowon, the military leader of the Nigerian Federation, and the
embossed slogans exhorting Nigerians to UNITY. So, in spite of
the rat-catcher, my antagonist, I know there is a specific history to
the formation of Nigerian identity, which includes this call to
UNITY. In the highly-charged atmospheres of fomenting national
identities, the need for a tragic art acquires a critical importance.

There are many obvious parallels for Nigeria in so critical a
process as the formation of a new nation state. In order to clarify
the importance of what Soyinka is doing, it would help to look at
the work of an Israeli theatre company, Tmu-Na, as it tests and
challenges the identity of its society. Their play, *Real Time*,[5] is set
in Tel Aviv on Yom Kippur – the Day of Atonement – with the 1973
Yom Kippur war about to break out. People gather in Eva's bar –
whereas Yom Kippur is that evening in the year normally kept for

family gatherings. These are lost characters, fragmented lives, drifting in and out of febrile relationships – delicate, fragile, breakable. As Israelis, they are brought together – in one nation – from many different cultures. The handyman sleeping rough in the bar remarks, 'In Russia I'm a Jew. Here, I'm just that Russian guy.' The actor, now an Israeli, is originally from Russia. The director, Nava Zukerman, herself of Polish extraction, comments in a programme note that, 'Every gesture used in performance is rooted in the individual experience of the performer.' The actors of the company draw on their real lives in making the play.

One of the characters, an Israeli woman, Eli, reappears in the bar after an unexplained absence in Europe. She describes, to the bar at large and, with considerable emotional pain, to the Czech lover whom she earlier abandoned, the experience of going to see an opera by Wagner in Berlin. 'It was,' she says, 'not easy to get tickets. An Israeli, a friend of an Israeli I knew, fixed it for me. What an opera hall! I wish *we* had such an opera hall here! *They* appreciate culture.' Inside the opera hall she sees a familiar face. Not that she knows the person, but, as she says, 'You know how it is. You immediately recognise *one of us!*' That is, an Israeli. 'Originally, he's from Czechoslovakia. He has a number on his arm—' Then, in what becomes a song of tragic love directed to her abandoned lover, Eli goes on to describe Wagner's opera, *Tannhäuser*. In Israel, Wagner's music is still redolent of Nazi Germany; it is anathema. Such a love song enters the concentration camps:

ELI: The last scene was the one. The only beautiful one. Suddenly, he understands that he loves her. Only her. And he runs and runs to tell her – *Ich liebe dich* – *Ich liebe dich* – I love you – Suddenly he stops. The stage is cut by a funeral procession. I didn't understand. She committed suicide. She committed suicide in the arms of his best friend. When he came it was already too late. And he stands there and sees her passing – dead. And it's already too late—. In every opera there is this moment. But I always wait for it. Even though I know—.

That is the tragedy for Eli, in the opera and in her life. That moment, of love, when she is already dead and the body cuts past him to the graveyard. And it is already too late. Eli's identification of herself and her Czech lover with the emotional deaths of the operatic lovers is complete. She is caught up in a fatalism held somewhere between exhaustion and rapture. In the Wagnerian tragedy of *Tannhäuser*, it is that moment of tragedy in the plot – irredeemable, inevitable. It is that moment we always wait for, even though we know it is going to happen. It is what happens every night the opera plays.

The problem in *Real Time* is how to locate this 'tragedy' within the context of the historical tragedy of the Holocaust. Eli's emotional rapture, *her* sense of the operatic tragedy, is sliced open by the intrusion of the – still difficult, still present – thought of the Holocaust: 'Not that it's not difficult for me to see Wagner in Berlin.' There are, it appears, two kinds of tragedy jarring against each other in the play. Like a blade, the thought of the Holocaust flashes through Eli's emotional response to Wagner's tragedy – the completeness of it, the strange security it seems to offer, its intransigence, in the way she holds to it and brings it into her relationships with the other people in the bar. She draws back from that moment of rapture.

If the emotional logic of Wagner's tragic opera is unnerved, the historical tragedy of the Holocaust is still at the heart of Israeli experience, and its consequences are being played out in *Real Time*. Time has stood still as far as the tattooed number on the arm, the ruptured lives and the tragedy of the Holocaust are concerned. It is present, and now. And again, it is the moment we are waiting for, even though we know it is going to happen. We know from the programme notes and we know historically that we are on the edge of the outbreak of the Yom Kippur war – of the fratricidal killing again. The characters in the bar in Tel Aviv, with their fractured relationships and their sense of being always on the precipice, the eve of war, are persecuted by this sense of imminent tragedy constantly replaying itself.

But what kind of tragedy, and what possible responses? If its emotional logic is tied to the coat-tails of Wagnerian folklore, Wagner's Germanic structures of feeling – intransigence, fatalism – *Real Time* is a devastating critique of Israeli society. But if there is a response to tragedy which, like Eli's thought of the Holocaust, can lead them to question their own self-persecutory relationships, they are loosed from a long nightmare. The play ends as the war begins, with tanks and planes rumbling on to the television set in the bar and each of the characters watching in silence.

The questions remain the same for *Madmen and Specialists* in the context of Nigerian drama, the creation of a Nigerian tragic art. How is the historical tragedy of Biafra to be located and explored in relation to the tensions and fragmentation inherent in the many peoples who go to make up Nigerian society? Wole Soyinka has made no secret of his assessment of the Biafran conflict as indeed the result of men's evil desires, rooted in a corrupt politics and presided over by genocides and demagogues in a climate of fear. In *The Man Died*,[6] the notes on his imprisonment during the war, Soyinka sets out his belief that, as distinct from the tyranny of states, '. . . it is essential to cling to the reality of peoples; these cannot vanish, they have no questionable *a priori* – they exist' (p. 175). *Madmen and Specialists*, like Tmu-Na's *Real Time*, explores the identities and relationships of people trying to pull their lives together. In Soyinka's play, this means literally trying to pull together the splintered fragments of their bodies:

> BERO: Father's assignment was to help the wounded readjust to the pieces and remnants of their bodies. Physically. Teach them to make baskets if they still had fingers. To use their mouths to ply needles if they had none, or use it to sing if their vocal cords had not been shot away . . .
>
> (p. 242)

It is in keeping with Soyinka's perception of the brutal power-lust of the forces behind the civil war that the leaders and healers in the play are perverted into madmen and specialists:

> BERO: He started well. But of course we didn't know which way his mind was working. Madmen have such diabolical cunning . . .
>
> (p. 237)

With a ferocious inter-personal ethos equated to cannibalism, this is not a tragedy to elicit the emotional rapture of fatalism, but fear of genocidal violence. For Soyinka, and for Nigeria, the problem is how to break, how purge this climate of fear?

It is worth returning to one more thing that the Israeli woman, Eli, says about the opera to her fellow Israelis – from all their different cultures:

> ELI: There was another beautiful scene there. The one he comes to ask her forgiveness. I don't understand German. But you have to admit, this anti-Semite made a beautiful music.

She hears the music, in its unreal beauty and its anti-Semitic, destructive implications – and still she can think of, and respond to, forgiveness. It must start somewhere. Eli is asking forgiveness in the bar; in *Tannhäuser*, the lover is asking forgiveness of the dead. The last word belongs to Soyinka's Blindman, speaking of Si Bero surrounded by the herbs she has gathered in a room against Bero's safe return, the striking sense of her as a *person*:

> BLINDMAN: I can only tell you what I felt – in that room where I stood with her. There is more love in there than you'll find in the arms of a hundred women. I don't know what you intend for her but . . .

> (p. 231)

Speaking as a Nigerian, in the context of the present nationalist disintegration in Bosnia, we in Nigeria should be warned and serious about this. A tragic art in theatre is not trivial as it traces the fault-lines, the cracks and tensions so often publicly, politically and personally unacknowledged in the society – the contaminating guilts. In real time the Biafran secession is not so far away. Another catastrophe should not just be that moment we always wait for, even though we know it's going to happen. It has a logic which must be repudiated by something more real in what we are capable of.

---

1 Don McCullin, 'Children of Biafra' in *Unreasonable Behaviour, An Autobiography*, London: Jonathan Cape (Vintage), 1992, pp. 123–5.

2 Wole Soyinka, *Madmen and Specialists* in *Collected Plays 2*, London: Oxford University Press, 1974, p. 236.

3 Wole Soyinka, *The Road* in *Collected Plays 1*, London: Oxford University Press, 1973.

4 Wole Soyinka, 'The Writer in a Modern African State' in *Art, Dialogue and Outrage*, Ibadan: New Horn Press, 1988, p. 18.

5 Tmu-Na, *Real Time*, performed in the Lyric Studio, Hammersmith, London, April 1993. All quotations provided orally to the present writer by the actors.

6 Wole Soyinka, *The Man Died: Prison Notes of Wole Soyinka*, London: Rex Collings, 1972.

On Being Squelched in the Spittle
of an Alien Race

MARTIN BANHAM

The words, of course, are Elesin's in *Death and the King's Horseman*.[1] Perhaps they invite us to look at the excuses given by Soyinka's characters for a failure to act, and offer us another – and neglected – recurrent theme in Soyinka's work, that of the failure of political will. The playwright's obsession with transition – the passage between the world of the living and the world of the ancestors – is as well documented as it is constantly intriguing, but what I would propose as a parallel concern of Soyinka's is more rarely identified by critics. And yet Soyinka has ludicrously been charged with standing apart from the political debate. I would argue that his work has constantly engaged with that debate by pointing to the failure of the post-independence generation of political leaders in Nigeria (and, of course, the reference is wider) to transcend the pleasures and corruptions of power. The theme is touched upon, implicitly if not explicitly, wherever we look in Soyinka's drama, starting – as do so many other strands in his work – in *A Dance of the Forests*, a comprehensive and extraordinarily predictive source work for his canon. Forest Head, in a play offered as an 'alternative' Independence celebration, despairs of those who celebrate their acquisition of power by turning away from the wisdom of the elders to suck ('squelch'?) up the privileges of the departing masters – the despair of the spiritual leaders expressed at the corruption of the secular:

> The fooleries of beings whom I have fashioned closer to me weary and distress me. Yet I must persist, knowing that nothing is ever altered. My secret is my eternal burden – to pierce the encrustations

of soul-deadening habit, and bare the mirror of original nakedness
. . . hoping that when I have tortured awareness from their souls,
that perhaps, only perhaps, in new beginnings . . .[2]

Brother Jero, that most perceptive and adaptable of men, could
contemptuously manipulate a politician whose ambitions were
shaped by alien parliamentary manners and the perks of high
office. It is no coincidence that Soyinka freely offered the manu-
script of *Jero's Metamorphosis* to whoever would wish to use it as a
brilliantly satirical recycling of Jero as the scavenger of political
garbage. Instances of those in power who manipulate it through
greed and abuse of their responsibilities abound in Soyinka's work,
whether amiably (the Bale Baroka in the idyllic fantasy of *The Lion
and the Jewel*) or grotesquely (Kadiye the 'fat' priest in the dark
pessimism of *The Swamp Dwellers*). *Kongi's Harvest* – perhaps the
most critically (and in performance) neglected of Soyinka's plays –
gives us not only the political charlatan Kongi himself, but also the
compromised spiritual leader, Oba Danlola. Daodu in *Kongi's
Harvest*, Olunde in *Death and the King's Horseman* and Eman in
The Strong Breed offer the possibility that the young can move
away from the circle of corruption, though not – especially in
Eman's case – without severe temptation. The theme can surely be
traced through all of Soyinka's other plays, more marginally
perhaps in that most 'transition' centred play *The Road* than in the
fierce post-detention *cri* of *Madmen and Specialists*, but flam-
boyantly proposed in *The Play of Giants*, *Opera Wonyosi* and
Requiem for a Futurologist, and touched on despairingly in *From
Zia with Love*. But nowhere is the theme more deliberately
pursued, I would suggest, than in *Death and the King's Horseman*.

I am always intrigued by the chronological placing of *Death and
the King's Horseman*. Soyinka's own sufferings in the Civil War are
graphically covered in his prison diaries, *The Man Died*. Connected
to them in mood, language and image is the 1971 *Madmen and
Specialists*, a bitter allegory depicting the military rulers of Nigeria
as cannibals feasting on the people, concluding with the powerful
spectre of Armageddon. This is a play of passionate anger and
despair, a play where language is often deliberately reduced from a
vehicle of logical communication to raw and crude sound-effect,

dislocated, disjointed, anthropoid. The play works theatrically as a total experience and not essentially as a developing narrative. The awful anger of the playwright is close to the surface of the play. By contrast, Soyinka's next play, *Death and the King's Horseman*, four years later in 1975, selects for the first time in the playwright's work a specific historical incident (one indeed earlier used by the Yoruba playwright Duro Ladipo in *Oba Waja*). There seems to be a conscious decision on the playwright's part to stand back from the destructive anguish of personal experience and to make his statement through the distancing device of the historical incident. The incident itself is as follows (and here I'm indebted to James Gibbs).[3] In December 1944 the Alafin of Oyo died. Oba Siyenbola Oladigbolu I had reigned for over thirty years. His senior minister, the Master of his Horse, Olokun Esin Jinadu, had a sacred duty to follow his dead king to the next world and the community anticipated his death. At the proper time – to be exact on 4 January 1945 – he dressed himself appropriately and, as Gibbs describes, began to dance through the streets on his way to his death. On hearing of this the British District Officer in Oyo intervened and ordered the detention of Olokun Esin. The ritual was therefore fatally interrupted and by implication the family of the king's horseman disgraced. At this point the Olokun Esin's son killed himself.

At first sight the play might seem to be an attack on the insensitivity of the British colonial authority in the face of a community ritual of extreme significance. Soyinka draws the District Officer and his wife, Simon and Jane Pilkings, as naive and ignorant, however well-meaning in their attitudes towards the culture in which they live. They are shown preparing to go to a fancy dress ball at the Residency dressed in Egungun masquerade costumes – a sacrilege in the eyes of the Yoruba as the Egungun are the awesome spirits of the ancestors. But Soyinka, in his introduction to the published play, specifically warns us against treating the play as one about the clash of cultures, and indeed though many aspects of British life in Nigeria are satirised in the play, there are also British characters who are shown to be acting courageously – especially a sea-captain who sacrifices his own life by taking a burning munitions ship out of Lagos harbour, making his own sacrifice for the good of the community in a telling parallel to events in Oyo. The colonial power is seen to be confused and bewildered by the culture over which it holds authority, and is certainly described as a corrupting influence. The son of the Elesin says to Mrs Pilkings: 'Your greatest art is the art of survival. But at least have the humility to let others survive in their own way'. His father excuses himself by claiming 'My will was squelched in the spittle of an alien race'. Of course like all fine works of literature this play is about many things, but my assertion would be that at the heart of it is an allegory about the lack of political will – the theme I believe Soyinka is constantly returning to – here most explicitly stated in the calm and rational exploration of an historical anecdote. The Elesin dons the appropriate costume and dances the appropriate steps: he has enjoyed the privileges of power but when the time comes to fulfil his duty to the community he is seen to be fatally flawed. Dancing through the market to his house of 'death' he shows disturbing signs of being too fond of this world to embrace the next, demanding gifts of cloth and finally the gift of a young bride. At the end of the play Elesin attempts to explain his actions to Iyaloja, the mother of the markets:

> My powers deserted me. My charms, my spells, even my voice lacked strength when I made to summon the powers that would lead me over the last measure of earth into the land of the fleshless. You saw it, Iyaloja. You saw me struggle to retrieve my will from the power of the stranger whose shadow fell across the doorway . . . (p. 68)

But Iyaloja dismisses Elesin's attempts to excuse himself because of the intervention of, by implication, the 'alien race', contrasting the expectations of the people with the behaviour of the king's minister:

> You have betrayed us. We fed you sweetmeats such as we hoped awaited you on the other side. But you said No, I must eat the world's left-overs. We said you were the hunter who brought the quarry down; to you belonged the vital portions of the game. No, you said, I am the hunter's dog and I shall eat the entrails of the

game and the faeces of the hunter . . . We said, the dew on earth's surface was for you to wash your feet along the slopes of honour. You said No, I shall step in the vomit of cats and the droppings of mice; I shall fight them for the left-overs of the world. (p. 68)

Soyinka speaks of the play's 'threnodic essence' – a lamentation for the dead. But it is also a lamentation for the living and, I would argue, carrying in addition to the metaphysical confrontation a parallel political confrontation – leaders destroying their people in their scramble for the left-overs of the world. Death and funerals are often Soyinka's images for the corrupt political world. On 29 June 1993 he wrote in anger and despair at the latest abuse of power in Nigeria:

When the National Electoral Commission of Nigeria decided, nearly two weeks ago, not to announce the verdict of the nation on the next civilian president, it did, in effect, pronounce a verdict on the Nigerian nation: a piecemeal death. The Chief Undertaker is General Ibrahim Babangida. The pall-bearers are the ethnic manipulators and arms dealers, self-styled latter-day patriots . . . The scavengers of history are hovering around the nation's borders . . . A nation of some 90 million people is being wound round the finger of a Master Player . . . His cohorts insist that the nation is on the path to democracy, but surely the signpost reads to all but the purblind: Transition to Hell.[4]

Forest Head, in a continuation of his lament quoted earlier in this essay, refers to his 'long-rumoured ineffectuality'. If Soyinka has been subject of the same rumour it is not because of the lack of clear and consistent political engagement in his work.

1 Wole Soyinka, *Death and the King's Horseman*, London: Methuen, 1975.

2 Wole Soyinka, *A Dance of the Forests* in *Collected Plays 1*, London: Oxford University Press, 1973, p. 71.

3 James Gibbs, *Wole Soyinka*, London: 1986.

4 Wole Soyinka in *The Independent*, London: 29 June 1993.

Against Ideology: Soyinka vs. Hunt

ADEWALE MAJA-PEARCE

A play, a novel, a poem, a painting or any other creative compo-
sition is *not a thesis on the ultimate condition of man* . . . To ask for a
'solid class perspective' in such a work curtails creative and critical
options and tries to dodge labour which properly belongs to the
socio-political analyst.

WOLE SOYINKA, Foreword to Opera Wonyosi

There is something poignant about the legion of Marxist critics who
invested so much intellectual and emotional capital arguing in
favour of the writer's commitment to an ideology that proved itself
so bankrupt so quickly, even if one's sympathies are necessarily
tempered by the underlying claim – hardly unique to the Marxists –
that art should serve the end of politics; that art *is* politics; and that
the writer who misses what seems to them a self-evident fact is
guilty of a species of 'romanticism'. Soyinka especially has been a
favourite target of those who demand that their literature conform
to what Farrukh Dhondy, writing in the wake of the Salman
Rushdie affair, has termed the 'onward-Christian-revolutionary-
Islamic-soldiers school of writing'.[1] One of the most thorough-
going of these is Geoffrey Hunt, the British critic, whose essay,
'Two African Aesthetics: Soyinka vs. Cabral', has since achieved a
certain notoriety.

Geoffrey Hunt, who defines romanticism as 'a cultural response
to collective insecurity',[2] castigates Soyinka for what he terms his
'inadequate conception of idology', and with it his related 'assumption' that 'commitment or ideology is something extraneous,
contingent or external. It is imagined that one's attitude to art

133

determines one's ideology when in reality it is one's ideology which shapes one's art'.[3] To clinch his argument, he singles out *The Man Died* (1972) – 'an overtly political work' – for particular mention, damning it as 'thin and personalized' because it never goes beyond 'the machinations of a Nigerian "Mafia" ':[4]

> [In the book] we find such statements as 'the revolutionary changes to which I have become more than ever dedicated . . .', 'For me, justice is the first condition of humanity', 'I did and still wish that the revolt in the West [of Nigeria] had achieved victory as a people's uprising'. But these pronouncements are not given any flesh. Instead there is the same lack of analysis, the same perplexing ambivalence about his political position.[5]

It says something about the power of received language, to say nothing of the rigs of the times, that dubious value judgements should pass so casually for genuine literary criticism; but it's doubtful, in any case, whether any writer could reasonably ignore a dressing-down cast in such condescending tones, particularly when the lecturer in question happens to be European and his pupil African. Such a heady combination of presumption and indelicacy goes a long way towards explaining Soyinka's lengthy response 'in kind', although he himself justifies the exercise on two counts: firstly, that 'in our own society, the printed word still carries some kind of mystique of its own'; secondly, that the tendency of foreign journals 'to make a beeline for the noisiest barrel' in their search for 'an "alternative view", a "controversial angle" ', confers on 'the *bolekeja* ['come down, let's fight'] squad' a spurious authority that cannot pass unchallenged.[6]

'The Autistic Hunt; or, How to Marximise Mediocrity' must easily rate as one of the most savage attacks ever launched by a writer on a 'virulent' critic, and we can judge the depth of Soyinka's rage by his 'regret that the epoch is gone when matters were settled in idioms other than words!'.[7] In the absence of pistols, however, words must suffice, although the subsequent charge of racism which Soyinka levels against his detractor in the course of his response – 'Our first task is to demolish, objectively, the pretensions of a racist critic'[8] – is hardly less violent in its implications. But the charge is unfortunate, and not only because it is untrue. We shall return to this presently; in the meantime, we are left with the ideologue's fatuous objections to Soyinka's prison memoir.

It ought to be said at once that *The Man Died* has been faulted on many grounds, including, as Geoffrey Hunt himself is quick to point out, the author's tendency to take 'petulant swipes at figures who are historically totally insignificant'.[9] This much is granted, even by Soyinka's most ardent admirers, but the book contains something infinitely more challenging than the dreary reiteration of a simple ideology, and nowhere more apparent than in the passage that the critic himself singles out as evidence of Soyinka's 'mystical holism':

> Militarist entrepreneurs and multiple dictatorships: this is bound to be the legacy of a war which is conducted on the present terms . . . The ramifications of a corrupt militarism and a rapacious mafia are endless and are nearly incurable. The war means a consolidation of crime, an acceptance of the scale of values that created the conflict, indeed an allegiance and enshrinement of that scale of values because it is now intimately bound to the sense of national identity.[10]

If this passage is to be held up as proof of Soyinka's misguided romanticism, of his 'lack of analysis' and his 'perplexing ambivalence', then it is at least arguable that the absence of any deeper moral dimension in the civil war writings by the overwhelming majority of Nigerian authors (the Marxists not excepted) contributed in some measure to the spiritual vacuum that enabled the ensuing decadence to flourish; but Soyinka's prophetic insight, which is even truer now than it was twenty years ago, is all the more remarkable against the background of his incarceration in Kaduna for the entire duration of the war – almost all of it in solitary confinement. It wasn't necessary to hang around the battle-front or gossip with colleagues in Lagos bars to gauge the true cost of the conflict. A simple newspaper cutting smuggled into his cell by a sympathetic prison guard was enough to tell him what he needed to know.

The cutting in question concerned the wedding of the Head of

State, General Yakubu 'Nero' Gowon, and the attendant celebrations that began in Lagos and proceeded in a northerly direction.
It obviously never occurred to the revellers that the populace for
whom all this was ostensibly being staged might be less than
enamoured at the evident waste, or even that the national imperative precluded celebrations of any kind; in the words of the
disillusioned prison guard: 'They say everybody economize. We no
fit pay school fee or buy uniform for picken. War dey war dey but dis
man bring all Lagos society come Kaduna . . . Wetin me get for in
wedding? Na me go fuck in wife?'.[11] So he hands over the
newspaper ('If you hear noise make you hide de paper for under our
pillow. A go take am when you finish. A no do dis work come kill
myself. I dey go sleep'), whereupon the prisoner discovers that the
fall of a Biafran town – Umuahia – has been hijacked by the proud
bridegroom as a wedding present to the dismembered nation:

> But the inside of the man, the deadness of mind and sense was
> summed up in the final unedifying revelation: that the taking of a
> rebel stronghold, the taking of even the smallest bow-and-arrow
> defended hamlet in a civil war was not to him the sum of lives on
> both sides, of mutilation and sacrifice, was not even the weighty
> dilemma and disquieting decisions of human sacrifice but – a
> wedding present! A glorification of a private and a personal bond
> between himself and some unknown, irrelevant quantity. Nothing
> but a feudal dynastic mentality could have conceived such irrever-
> ence, nothing but power drunkenness could have bilged forth such
> grandiloquent vomit on the entire national sacrifice.[12]

One would have to search hard indeed for a more overtly political
statement in the entire corpus of modern Nigerian literature, and
political in a deeper because more inclusive sense than is contained
in the work of those in possession of a more overtly political
agenda. In one of the lectures collected in *Myth, Literature and the
African World* (1976), delivered at the University of Cambridge
following his release and self-exile, Soyinka himself readily con-
cedes the existence in his own work of what he terms a 'social
vision':

Asked recently whether or not I accepted the necessity for a literary ideology, I found myself predictably examining the problem from the inside, that is, from within the consciousness of the artist in the process of creating . . . My response was – a social vision, yes, but not a literary ideology. Generally the question reflects the preoccupation, neither of the traditional nor the contemporary writer in African society *but of the analyst after the event, the critic.* [My italics.][13]

The distinction, of course, is everything. A social vision – defined in the same essay as a 'creative concern which conceptualises or extends actuality beyond the purely narrative, making it reveal realities beyond the immediately attainable, a concern which upsets orthodox acceptances in an effort to free society of historical or other superstitions',[14] – is not in itself a prerequisite for judging the relative merits of a given piece of work. Alex La Guma's *A Walk in the Night*, for instance, which 'makes no social visionary claims but restricts itself to a near obsessive delineation of the physical, particularised reality of a South African ghetto existence', nevertheless provides a 'profound and disturbing insight into humanity'.[15] Conversely, both William Conton's *The African* and Lewis Nkosi's *Rhythms of Violence*, aspiring as they do to 'reveal realities beyond the immediately attainable',[16] simply degenerate into a mawkish sentimentality, the one acting as a piece of cheap propaganda for an imperfectly understood Christianity, the other displaying 'a total alienation from reality and a misunderstanding of the nature and demands of true tragedy'.[17] The 'warning' to the 'would-be social visionary' is spelled out clearly enough:

But writing directed at the product of a social matrix must expect to remain within it, and to resolve the conflicts that belong to that milieu by the logical interactions of its components, one cannot stand outside it all and impose a pietistic resolution plucked from some rare region of the artist's uncontaminated soul.[18]

A social vision, in short, is not the same thing as an ideology, the point being that Soyinka, the creative artist, unlike Geoffrey Hunt, the hidebound critic, does not need to experience the world according to a ready-made blueprint. It would probably be futile to go further and say that the tag of romanticism, to the extent that it constitutes 'the ultimate, capital crime in the arts' to begin with,[19] is better applied to Marxist ideologues, whose own 'collective in-security' in the face of life's imponderables, including 'how they eat, laugh, play, woo and even make love',[20] drives them to find answers in a mythology that is every bit as esoteric as that which they purport to despise. For the believer, of course, a mythology works to the extent that it is a true and literal description of the world, which is why Soyinka's charge of racism is at odds with what we know about Geoffrey Hunt's particular mythology.

Soyinka identifies the key to the critic's 'racist clownery' in a passage in which Geoffrey Hunt suggests that the European colonisation of Africa was made possible by reason of its superior civilisation:

> . . . Soyinka reproaches the Nigerian poet and dramatist Femi Osofisan for making the point that animism accommodates natural disaster and so negates social action for improvement ['Because the animist world accommodates and sublimates disaster within the matrix of ritual, the Red Indian world collapsed, and so did ours . . .'], or to put it in Soyinkese: 'the Marxist view of man and history, denounces the insidious enervation of the social will by the tragic afflatus'. Soyinka's response to the 'Marxist view' is: 'A little more gunpowder and, not only the natives of South America but their brothers in the North would have wiped out the white invaders.' What he does not ask is what kind of social organization and associated culture and beliefs make gunpowder *possible*? To provide a parody as an answer, let us imagine, for instance, Australian Aborigine hunter-gatherers running after small game with boomerangs all day to hurry home to quadrophonic Stockhausen in carpeted high-rise apartments as the 4:30 work siren sounds across the desert.[21]

The 'parody' is unfortunate, even 'thick-skinned', but hardly 'racist'. Nor is it answered by claiming that the boomerang 'is one of the most intriguing and, even today, challenging examples of aerodynamic technology',[22] which may or may not be true, but which, coming perilously close as it does to special pleading, is in any case irrelevant to Geoffrey Hunt's argument. Worse yet, the charge of racism conveniently overlooks a central axiom of Geoffrey Hunt's ideology, and which Hunt himself spells out in unambiguous terms:

> We should approach Soyinka's concept of 'race' through the concept of 'class'. 'Class' has an objective existence in the essential relations of production . . .; it is primary, historical and universal. 'Race', on the other hand (when it is not being used in the strictly biological sense . . .) is a subjective response to an objective class situation . . .[23]

Whatever one's reservations about the analysis of Nigerian society – of *any* society – based on the concept of 'class', there is no intrinsic reason to doubt Hunt's sincerity in rejecting the notion of 'race' outside the strictly biological, such a rejection itself comprising at least part of the Marxist appeal to any number of African intellectuals attempting to understand the 'objective' historical forces that have placed them in a debilitating relationship *vis-à-vis* Europe.

'Race does not exist outside men's minds,'[24] Geoffrey Hunt asserts, and in this he is not only consistent in terms of his ideology, but entirely right in *human* terms. There is no such thing as 'race' for as long as it devolves on what James Baldwin has called 'the legend of color' (which is all that we are left with), any such definition being 'humanly impossible': '*Humanly* does not refer to the virtues but the possibilities, or limits, of the human being. People can be defined by their color only by the beholder, who, in order to arrive at this definition, must will himself/herself blind'.[25] For Soyinka, however, Geoffrey Hunt's 'fatuous claim'

> . . . is possible only from a racist conniver, by which we mean, one who, for reasons which are to be found in his own racial temper, seeks to undermine the racial security of others. We do not claim anywhere that social progress should be dependent on the racial factor . . . No, we claim merely that race can be objectively

discussed and that the racial factor in culture need not be obscured, else, the discussion of culture remains incomplete.[26]

On the contrary, it is 'the racial factor' which obscures the discussion of culture; and to the extent that it is a necessary component of a transcendent African literature, of a literature of social vision, so does Soyinka do violence to his own achievement as a writer whose work has always striven to 'reveal realities beyond the immediately attainable'. In the process, the reductive notion of race itself becomes just another ideology that is every bit as invidious for the creative artist as that which he seeks to undermine.

1 Farrukh Dhondy, 'A Satanic Sermon', *Index on Censorship*, 5/1989, p. 42.

2 Geoffrey Hunt, 'Two African Aesthetics: Soyinka vs. Cabral', in *Marxism and African Literature*, ed. Georg M. Gugelberger, London: James Currey, 1985, p. 64.

3 Ibid, p. 83.

4 Ibid, p. 82.

5 Ibid, p. 85.

6 Wole Soyinka, 'Responses in Kind', in *Art, Dialogue and Outrage: Essays on Literature and Culture*, Ibadan: New Horn Press, 1988, p. 268.

7 Wole Soyinka, 'The Autistic Hunt; or, How to Marximise Mediocrity', in *Art, Dialogue and Outrage*, ibid, p. 292.

8 Ibid, p. 280.

9 Geoffrey Hunt, op. cit, p. 82.

10 Wole Soyinka, *The Man Died*, London: Rex Collings, 1972; Penguin Books, 1975, p. 182.

11 Ibid, p. 233.

12 Ibid, p. 235.

13 Wole Soyinka, *Myth, Literature and the African World*, Cambridge: Cambridge University Press, 1976, p. 61.

14 Ibid, p. 66.

15 Ibid, p. 65.

16 Ibid, p. 66.

17 Ibid, p. 71.

18 Ibid, p. 73.

19 'We will not yet depart from the issue of romanticism – which, by the way, I am far from conceding the ultimate, capital crime in the arts, seeing in it only a tendency to be noted where it occurs, and its thematic appropriateness objectively debated.' Wole Soyinka, 'The Autistic Hunt', op. cit., p. 286.

20 'The means of life, and how they are produced, exchanged and shared out and the social institutions that the whole process gives rise to do move men, do profoundly affect the very quality of their lives: how they eat, laugh, play, woo and even make love. This universe – of moral significance of values and the quality of human life – is what imaginative literature is about.' Ngũgĩ wa Thiong'o, 'Writers in Politics', in *Writers in Politics*, London: James Currey, 1981, pp. 71–72.

21 Geoffrey Hunt, op. cit., p. 76.

22 Wole Soyinka, 'The Autistic Hunt', op. cit., p. 281.

23 Geoffrey Hunt, op. cit., p. 80.

24 This formulation appeared in an earlier draft of Hunt's essay. He omits it from the published version. Soyinka, who was responding to the draft essay, quotes it in his own response (p. 307).

25 James Baldwin, *Evidence of Things Not Seen*, London: Michael Joseph, 1985, pp. 99–100.

26 Wole Soyinka, 'The Autistic Hunt', op. cit., p. 307.

Wole Soyinka Interviewed
3 July 1993, Notting Hill Gate, London

'BIYI BANDELE-THOMAS

'Biyi Bandele-Thomas: *Earlier this year you were accosted at Murtala Muhammed International Airport in Lagos and delayed by men from the State Security Service (SSS). What happened?*

Wole Soyinka: This was in January. I was on my way to Paris. Ironically, it was a trip in which the Nigerian government was participating and arranged by the Franco-Nigerian Association. A book of photographs for which I'd written captions was to be launched, and the pictures were to be exhibited; it was to be a travelling exhibition, showing Nigeria in a very positive light apart from the usual things people hear about. This was the idea. The Nigerian Ambassador to France was to be present, there was to be a symposium lasting an entire week; it was to be opened by the mayor of one of the Paris *arrondissements*. It was a high-level official engagement. Anyway, I got to the airport and – there's always an SSS man in the immigration booth – as soon as I arrived and presented my passport, the man said, 'Oh, could you come with us please'. So I followed them. I'd checked in, of course. They asked me to go and retrieve my luggage, which was by this time sitting on the tarmac for the security identification before the passengers board. As soon as that happened, I said to him, 'Listen, if you people mess around with me, I will not travel, I want you to understand that.' He said, 'We won't keep you long.' So I went along, picked up my luggage, and followed the officers to their room. We got in there and they began taking my luggage to pieces, shook out all my files, picked up my trousers, felt along the hems. It was quite thorough. They went through everything. This lasted about an hour. There was a television on in the room, there was a wrestling event going on, so I sat with my eyes glued to the television. And they said, 'Oh, Professor Soyinka, you have to watch us inspecting these things.' I said, 'You can stuff anything you like in there. I haven't got the slightest interest. Just hurry up with what you're doing, find whatever you want to find, because I'm going home.' Let's say the plane was due to leave at 11.35. At 11.32 they completed their search. In the meantime, somebody was standing there, holding a telephone conversation with somebody else somewhere. I presume that orders were given that, OK, you can let him go now. So they then packed my things back, gave me my passport, and said I was free to travel. I said, 'You're crazy. You think I came to the airport to start chasing aeroplanes on the tarmac?' They said, 'No, no, no, we'll take you to the tarmac.' I said, 'No way, I'm going back home.' And that's exactly what I did.

BB-T: *You've had several confrontations with this government in the past. But this is a new development in your relationship with them.*

WS: It's an escalation. I've had veiled threats, I've had reports – they have their own SSS, I have my own SSS. They have several grades, watch grades, either on A or B or C. And I've been moving from A to B to C, back to A. In other words, one means: report his movements; another means: ask one or two questions, find out what he is doing, who he's seeing. Another grade – even higher – means: see if you can furtively search his papers. And then of course you get to the grade where you are absolutely persecuted; and, finally, there's the topmost grade where, after searching you and so forth, you're *not* allowed to travel. One of these grades, the subtle one, was applied to Obasanjo[1] himself not so long ago. He travels on a diplomatic passport, or rather, he did. I haven't checked the story with him directly, but someone who is close to him told me. And they successfully *lost* his passport at the airport and he couldn't travel. Somehow, his passport just vanished. For two hours the plane was held up for him. For two hours he could not travel . . . I've been on the receiving end of various levels of attention but this was the first time it really flared up into the open. My wife also was harassed. This was in June. She was flying to the

US to join me in Harvard where I was to receive a doctorate. At the airport, the moment they saw the name, they said, 'Madam, come this way'. They took her to the same interrogation room, asked her all sorts of stupid questions: 'Where's your husband?' 'Why are you not travelling with him?' 'You say you're a journalist on your passport but on the form you wrote something different.' She said, 'Look, I'm not a practising journalist right now, but I *am* a journalist.' You know, real idiotic, moronic questions like that. Just to delay her and try and get her to miss the plane, or whatever. Anyway, just before the plane left they released her.

BB-T: *In 1960, when* A Dance of the Forests *was produced to mark Nigeria's Independence celebrations, did you look into the future and see us not only leading from the rear but being also the most politically and economically abused entity in what you've described somewhere as 'a benighted continent, now mangled beyond hope'?*

WS: Let me tell you what happened to me during my studies in England. My focus was very much on South Africa. I took Independence very much for granted. I was not overly excited about Independence movements for the simple reason that it seemed so obvious to me that when people are on top of you, you're going to throw them off. I took it for granted that that had to happen. In some cases, I saw that it was already happening. In Kenya, unfortunately, I saw that this would be a bloody process. In West Africa, I didn't see it as being a bloody process. There were already these various movements including . . . I mean, there were occupational hazards, people like Enahoro were going to jail for alleged sedition against the colonial government. But, for me, this was part of the excitement of de-colonisation, of Independence. So my attention was focused very much on South Africa. I was really obsessed with the Apartheid situation at the time, and of course with Kenya, where the Mau-Mau struggle was just commencing. It took me a while – and I know exactly how it happened – to begin to focus on the kind of philosophy which would replace the colonial relationship with the Africans. It was a single moment at one of the earliest stages of our semi-Independence when the first ministers arrived in England. I remember that a group of us went to meet them wanting to discuss issues. We were all excited that we were going to come home to an independent country, full of creative excitement, we already saw visions of an African paradise showing these bloody colonial people what energy they'd been suppressing. And we came and met these ministers. Within five minutes, I knew that we were in serious trouble. It was clear that they were more concerned with the mechanisms for stepping into the shoes of the departing colonial masters, enjoying the same privileges, inserting themselves in that axial position towards the rest of the community. I saw the most naked and brutal signs of alienation of the ruler from the ruled, from the very first crop. There were one or two exceptions, of course. And then I realised that the enemy within was going to be far more problematic than the external, easily recognisable enemy. And that was when I began to write *A Dance of the Forests*. It was then I began to recollect, to say to myself: well, what's so surprising about that? Why should we expect it to be different? After all, we participated in certain crimes against ourselves, we participated in enslaving our own kind. So, why shouldn't it happen all over again? That's when I began to pay very serious attention to what I saw as a budding dictatorial mentality. These new leaders were alienated, that was the main theme of *A Dance of the Forests*.

BB-T: *Three decades on, your misgivings have been confirmed?*

WS: Brutally so, brutally so. I wish they weren't, I wish I'd been proved wrong. But, unfortunately, all across the continent they've been confirmed.

BB-T: *Let's move to the present: what are your reactions to the cancellation of the 1993 elections in Nigeria?*

WS: Well, for me this has been one of the greatest blows to the development of Nigeria as a nation. It has nothing to do with the whole transition programme, which was flawed from the very beginning, including the creation of both the parties by the military. But as I've said in the past, this was something that one could live with as long as the progressive movement within the country could co-ordinate its energies and seize the structure of one of the parties then there might be hope. But of course when the government then proceeded to write the manifestos for both parties, then the whole thing was over. But even so, Nigerians made up their minds that even a mouldy loaf of bread was better than nothing. And that the immediate target, the short term goal for the Nigerian polity, was to get rid of the military. So, everybody mobilised, including those in the political class as well as those who were normally politically comatose, if this was one way of getting rid of the government. Now, eventually, something interesting developed, after all the cancellations, the changes, the banning and unbanning; all the tortuous, contradictory motions of Babangida's regime. Finally, two candidates emerged for the presidential elections. And the results – leaving aside personalities – were such that they created a certain kind of optimism for what has been the goal of Nigerians – at least, thinking and de-tribalised, de-sectionalised Nigerians – just to have a candidate who could command support across the country. And if you examine Abiola's results there's no question at all that he succeeded in doing this. From Kano to Lagos, to Ondo, Kwara, even Bauchi, he gained 44 per cent of the votes cast. And this, for me, was one silver lining in the horrendously dark clouds which had been cast over the nation by Babangida's tricks and wiles and mismanagement of the country and the sinister designs which he seemed to have on the country. And to have those elections cancelled went beyond even the denial of the democratic expression of the people. It went beyond it. The results were halfway announced . . . But obviously the calculations of the Babangida regime had gone wrong. This regime clearly did not expect Abiola to do so well, so they began to improvise at the expense of the nation. And by expense I mean both monetary expense as well as the psychological and political investment. This single man, with a small cutlery, decided to defy the will of Nigerians. It's a huge set-back for the entire democratic process.

BB-T: *In an article which appeared both in the* Guardian *and the* New York Times *you use a proverb to illustrate what you've described as Babangida's bias in these elections. You wrote 'Whose* *cause will the housefly promote if not that of the leg riddled with sores?'*

WS: Well, it's this way: the military regime, Babangida's regime, obviously favoured Tofa, and the reason is not far to seek. Tofa was the person who first flew the kite of the Babangida-Must-Stay campaign. He was the one who wrote an article two years ago saying that Babangida should stay until the year 2000. He was totally unknown. Tofa *Who*? That was the question on everybody's lips: Tofa *Who*? I know that this article was not written by Tofa. It was written by the *éminence grise* in the Security Services whom I will not name for the moment but who has been masterminding the entire prolongation programme of the regime. It was written for Tofa by this individual to begin the process of persuading Babangida to stay. The whole thing has been stage-managed from the word go. This regime wanted somebody it could continue to manipulate and Tofa fitted the bill. In addition to that, there were other scenarios waiting to be played. Now it turns out that there are affidavits against Tofa suggesting that he's not fit to be president on moral grounds. So this card was also in the hands of this regime to play. Where the calculation went wrong was the victory of Abiola. And so they had to go to the extent of not merely annulling the elections, but creating new rules to ensure that the two candidates could not compete. Of course, they had to be even-handed; they had to disqualify Tofa also. So what do you do? You cancel the elections and then you create rules which make sure that the finalists cannot re-enter the race, then you proceed to unban those whom you had banned before! This is toying with the nation, this is a diabolical game being played with the destiny of at least 90 million people by the small caucus – fifteen at most – who meet and decide these things. We know most of them. They sit down and cook up this witches' broth with which they poison the entire nation. It's the most callous disregard of law, of equity, of justice, of common-sense, and it's a mark of contempt for a nation which is so full of human and material potential. I've never heard the like of this before. We must search the history books, we must search the whole history of elections and see if any country can come up with something of this nature. It offends any kind of juridical process.

BB-T: *What implications do you foresee as a result of the cancellation?*

WS: The scenario is not very pleasant. First of all, there will be a successful boycott which will make nonsense of the next electoral process if it does take place. Now what happens then: the only justification for the boycott is that a choice has already been made, and that a fair number of Nigerians recognise one president. So, Babangida goes ahead and holds this other election and some kind of president emerges. So you have a Zairean situation in which there are two prime ministers. But the Nigerian situation is far more serious because we have an electoral process and the people have made their choice. Worse yet, we have a situation where the army has shown obvious signs of disaffection with Babangida's manipulations. So you have a divided army, you have a divided nation, and all because of the – I can't even call it megalomania – of the quirks, of the irrationality of one individual and his tiny junta. It's not a pleasant prospect, I'm afraid, for Nigeria. The only rational and patriotic course is for Babangida, who created this mess, to respect the wishes expressed by the people *under* the rules which he himself set. This is the most painful part of it. This man laid out the rules, people reluctantly accepted these rules, and now he's been defeated by his own rules. And yet he insists that he wants to start all over again. It's too preposterous.

BB-T: *There have been rumours that Abiola has been placed under house arrest. Any fears for his safety?*

WS: I've been away a week. I've been on the phone and nobody has been able to confirm that. One solution for the other side is just to eliminate him. You eliminate him, part of the problem is solved: there's no more reason to boycott elections, you can't insist on him being president, that's it. So Abiola's security is paramount right now. Ironically, when I was trying to persuade him, I didn't realise that I should be bothering about my own security. It was a few days later that the helicopters came, circled my house, and took off back to Lagos. Their mission was to tell me that they were around, that Big Brother had eyes everywhere.

BB-T: *In your article in the* Independent *you equate these events to a murder; you describe the killing of Nigeria, and you say that 'the pall-bearers are the ethnic manipulators and arms dealers, self-styled latter-day patriots'. One of those to whom you refer is Arthur Nzeribe,[2] who is known to be incredibly wealthy, albeit through arms-dealing. What has he to gain by contriving to have the military in power in perpetuity?*

WS: Well, I don't know if you've read Arthur Nzeribe's book.[3] It gives a very interesting insight into the mind of the man. This is a man who desperately needs to be relevant. He needs to be *knowing*, to be inside the action. It's a compulsion. If he's not centre-stage politically, he likes it to be known that he's backstage. He has to have had a hand in every political pie, whether military or civilian. He exaggerates his role in many things. It's a very revealing book, and of course *this* has given him an opportunity actually to be *seen*, actually to act out some of the fantasies which are already expressed in that book. So, there is a kind of schoolboy immaturity in Arthur Nzeribe. It doesn't matter what role he's playing as long as he's playing it and he's being seen to play it. He is a psychological study, and this is why he's been able to team up with our Grey Eminence in the Security. Now, *he*, the nameless one, he set up the Third Eye Movement, a pro-government thing which now runs its own newspaper.

BB-T: *What's that called?*

WS: *The Third Eye.* There's no question at all that the two came together for a common purpose, and that some of the finance came from the Security Services. Nzeribe became the culmination of these various moves including, for instance, the insertion of editorials in the government-owned newspapers, the *Daily Times* and the *New Nigerian*. All these were either instigated by this man or even partly written by him. You must have read about the resignation of Abdulazeez, editor of the *New Nigerian*, which just confirmed what we'd been saying all along, that many of these editorials came from the presidency. Either from the Secret Service or, latterly, from the pen of Mr Chukwumerijie, *Comrade* Chukwumerijie, the Secretary for Information. Abdulazeez alleged that Chukwumerijie faxed an editorial from Abuja which they used in *New Nigerian* which said, in effect, that there is a third party – which was Nzeribe's, the Party of Twenty-Five Million Signatories – and that Nigerians have to realise that there is a third party. It's an editorial which, of course, was calling for the cancellation of the elections. Saying that since such a large proportion of people boycotted it, blablabla . . .

BB-T: *Did some people boycott the elections?*

WS: No, it's a lie, it's a lie. When they say some people did not hear about the announcement that the elections would take place eventually, the question in my mind is, how did they hear about the original court injunction? If communication was so bad; if the people in the rural areas couldn't hear Nwosu[4] say that they should go and vote, how come they heard about the court injunction? These people are liars, they don't even deserve to be taken seriously. That's the whole story of the Babangida-Must-Stay story. It's complete orchestration from the Security Service.

BB-T: *Chinua Achebe wrote last year in an article in the* Guardian *'I found it difficult to forgive Nigeria and my countrymen and women for the nonchalance and cruelty that unleashed upon us these terrible events which set us back a whole generation and robbed us of the chance to be a medium rank developed nation in the 20th century.' Do you share these sentiments? Is it not true that 'those terrible events' were possibly partly because of what you yourself have described as the abdication of the role of thinker by intellectuals, by the intelligentsia?*

WS: We have missed many chances. You know my position about the Civil War, of course. I believe that the war should never have been fought. And I blame, equally, both the so-called Nigerian side and the so-called Biafran side. And when we say blame, we are talking about the leadership at crucial moments. But we are also talking about leadership even during non-crucial moments. During the period of possible recovery, for instance, Gowon wasted many years of development. Then we, the populace, wasted chances by failing to choose the right leadership when we had the chance. Shagari[5] was a disaster. Not even those who praise his character, his personality, tolerance, whatever that means . . . not even his greatest admirers would deny that he was a disaster for the nation in terms of policy decisions implementation. His reign was a zero, a minus.

BB-T: *But Shagari was allegedly 'installed' by Obasanjo.*

WS: Well, I was in the thick of the '83 election. I was not so much in the thick of the '79 elections, although I was involved in some serious monitoring. In fact, I was a polling agent for Bola Ige in one or two places, and I was certainly at the nerve centre of some of the monitoring of that. I remember phoning Bisi Onabanjo[6] and reporting certain events which were taking place in Kaduna with the connivance of the military. I for one do not accept Obasanjo's denial of having had a hand in the installation of Shagari. And of course the whole business of the two-third formula, the appointment of a Chief Justice just before the elections, the revelations about Shagari, even before he became president, of being involved in the choice of this Chief Justice who was later to adjudicate when Shagari's presidency was contested in court . . . These allegations have to be answered very concretely before I can accept the professed innocence of Obasanjo about handing over the country to Shagari. Quite apart from the electoral malpractices, *serious* electoral malpractices which were actually carried out by soldiers who were taking orders from Lagos.

We the intellectuals, the creative people, what is our own culpability in all of this? Well, depending on what mood I'm in, I've been inclined sometimes to excoriate the entire tribe of intellectuals. But when I look, comparatively, at what really our capability has been, what capacity we *have* in the profession we've chosen in that aspect of our relationship to the rest of society, we're not really a potent lot. We're basically an impotent lot. All we can do is intervene with ideas, and I know that those who've been governing us have never really been short of ideas proffered to them by very serious and dedicated intellectuals. At the same time, of course, there have been the intellectuals of the Establishment, whether in the economic field or in the political field, but ultimately the responsibility is leadership. Those who either seize leadership or have leadership conferred on them. They make the choice. They make the choice between the different sets of intellectuals. And they must live with it, they must bear the ultimate responsibility. The intellectuals are *not* in power. So, I would like to limit our level of culpability to the fact that we are divided; that we have too many sycophants among us.

BB-T: *Now, to this question of being Nigerian. Is the statement, 'I am a Nigerian' not, at best, an acknowledgement of the fact that I have to carry a passport which bears that description, and, at worst, an abstract and absolutely meaningless statement? Would it not be more honest to say, I am Hausa, or I'm Ibibio, or I'm Yoruba . . . isn't there a very strong argument for a confederacy within this geo-political entity known as Nigeria?*

WS: It's a very troubling question. During the Civil War, I'm on record as having said that I'd rather Biafra broke away and created its own entity than have Nigeria stay together at the price that it must pay – especially the future consequences of that price, because that kind of price, you don't pay it once and for all. The ramifications carry on for quite a long time. I described the secession of Biafra as being *morally justified but politically erroneous*. I used that very expression. I distinguished between them because I felt that a moral situation had been created which justified any decision of Biafra to seek to be a separate entity. But I felt that it was a political error because of the circumstances of the world, and the circumstances of Nigeria within the African situation. There was also a political error in the fact that when Biafra seceded it failed to recognise the rights of its own minorities to choose where they wanted to be. Whether to be on their own or to be with Nigeria. I've given that background to underscore the fact that I understand that feeling, that question which all but political demagogues must be able to tackle honestly.

Do I want Nigeria to remain one? Do I prefer it to remain a Nigeria as presently defined, or do I prefer something else? I'm going to leave that aside, for now. I'm talking about a kind of demagogic position which says there's an entity called Nigeria and that entity is sacrosanct. I find that a most ridiculous statement. When did Nigeria as a nation come into being? And how did it come into being? Nigeria was an artificial creation, and it was a creation which did not take into consideration either the wishes or the will *or* the interests of the people who were enclosed within that boundary. They were lumped together. So, the genesis of Nigeria, as with many African countries, is very flawed, to start with. In fact, I remember that when the OAU adopted as one of its canons the notion of the sacrosanctity of the colonially inherited territorial boundaries, I said, 'Oh my God'. My statement then was that I would have thought that the sensible thing would be for the OAU to sit down with square rule and compass and *re-draw* the boundaries.

BB-T: *Do you think that is feasible?*

WS: No no no, it's no longer feasible. But at that time, before independent economic units *congealed* and became difficult to break, it was – for me – not only politically right but economically and psychologically viable to re-define our destiny. We want, in effect, to be re-born along the decisions of our political will. It would have been an act of enormous political strength and determination. If the Europeans can come and do that for us, why could we not have seized our chance to do it for ourselves? So, in principle, I recognise and accept the kind of statement which says just what is Nigeria, anyway? I don't understand it, I know that I am a Yoruba, I know that I am a Hausa, I know I am an Efik . . . I understand that statement. On the other hand, unrolling of historical events, the sharing of certain experiences, political fortunes, economic arrangements, cultural relations, cultural inter-action, can itself create a feeling of oneness within even the most artificial of boundaries, and so over a few generations it is possible, I think, for one to begin to feel proud of the cultural riches of Kaduna, or Maiduguri even though one is from Aba or Ife.

BB-T: *I was born in the north, in Kafanchan, and raised in Kaduna, Bauchi, Jos, Kano . . . all over the north, for the first eighteen years of my life. My parents are Yoruba, and when I went to my father's home town for the first time I was a teenager. I felt like a total stranger and spoke with an accent. Hausa was, basically, my first language. As far as I was concerned (and this applied to my sisters and brothers as well), I was born in the north. I'm Hausa. And then I finished secondary school, got very good results and tried to get a place at Bayero University, Kano. I was turned down, I later found out, because of my name. That, for me, was a revelation. I was being told, go back to where your parents are from. Not in so many words, but . . .*

WS: I'm very glad you mentioned that experience because such experiences, which affect hundreds of thousands of Nigerians in a very visceral way, militate against that sense of oneness which one is talking about. Let me support that with an incident which I know very well. I once attacked publicly the former Minister of Education, Jubril Aminu, who one day, when he was Minister of Education, just repatriated all southern principals from northern schools. One of them was my landlady. She was in the north somewhere, and she'd been there for years, she'd made friends, she was very much at home. In fact, she used to joke that she was so close to the local chief that they used to call her his girlfriend. That's how integrated she was. Now, how do you expect people to respond to that? They've been told, 'You're not part of this section of the country', which means Nigeria is being *differently* defined from what they had always believed.

BB-T: *A few years ago, a prominent Nigerian politician, Sam Mbakwe, called for the return of the British. Earlier this year, an American academic writing in the* New York Times *– I believe – also made a strong argument for a return to the days of Empire. 'Let's* *face it,'* he wrote, *'some countries are just not fit to govern themselves.'*

WS: My answer to that is that what Europe is discovering these days is that they too have never been fit to govern themselves. And they only survived because they had ruthless tyrants. In other words, all these years, all these decades, these countries have never really governed themselves. They've succeeded in staying together and progressing in one way or the other – and even that progress is questionable these days – only because they were being governed by an alien, what I call Alienated Power: Ceauşescu, Hoxha of Albania, Stalin and his successors in the Soviet Union. In other words, these people have never governed themselves. And the moment they had the chance to govern themselves, see what's been happening. This relates also of course to the sense of nationality. It throws into question the whole sense of homogeneity –

BB-T: *I was going to ask also what you think we have to learn, if there is anything to learn, from what's happened in former Yugoslavia.*

WS: It's back to my old position – what is happening in former Yugoslavia is, for me, too heavy a price to pay for the abstract concept of national unity. And, Nigeria should learn that some sacred notions, when confronted by not-so-sacred reality, should be re-examined. If the cost to Nigeria is the price being paid by Yugoslavia or Somalia, then I think we had all better sit round the table and re-examine that concept. It's not just Yugoslavia – we tend to forget scenarios like the brutal civil war which has been going on in Sudan for over twenty years. Now, I think that statement, the statement of a twenty-year-old civil war is clear and unambiguous. I am most impressed by John Garang's group who, at the last meeting, said, 'Look, we're not asking for the dismemberment of Sudan; we're not saying that we want to secede; we are just saying that we do not want to be governed by the Sharia Laws, and that if that obstacle is removed, we're quite willing to be integrated in a particular relationship with the rest of the country.' To me, that's a very generous statement, because the *statement* of a twenty-year-old civil war is so unambiguous: it says we don't belong together. That's all.

BB-T: *Do you think that a confederacy would be a solution?*

WS: I think that would be a solution for Sudan.

BB-T: *And for Nigeria?*

WS: Well, if the worst-case scenario – which is very possible in the present Nigerian circumstances – starts to unfold, I certainly would not be averse to a confederacy. It's, for me, not the ideal, but if that worst-case scenario is what may result from this situation in which we have a divided army that is allied with those atavistic, tribalistic forces which will not accept leadership except *from* their own section, then I don't see why the innocent people in Nigeria should pay the penalty for the short-sightedness of a small group of people. And we know that the blunder of one individual in this kind of situation can mean tragedy for hundreds of thousands of people.

BB-T: *Some commentators have said – and maybe it's a simplistic theory – that if Nigeria's relatively sizeable number of very wealthy people were to come together and invest in Nigeria as they would in a business enterprise, that not only would Nigeria be able to pay off its foreign debts but it might also become a viable entity.*

WS: I'm not in possession of facts and figures but I'm inclined to accept that statement. This may be one of the losses which Nigeria will sustain by not having somebody like Abiola at the helm of affairs. Abiola is a very capable businessman. Some people say he acquired his wealth crookedly and that he is in league with multi-national corporations and so on and so forth, but all I can say is give me a competent crook rather than an incompetent, inept angel. Especially when you are dealing with a vast and complex country like Nigeria, which has enormous resources, for heaven's sake. It hurts, each time I travel out, to see how much these people here have succeeded where we have failed. If we didn't have the resources it wouldn't hurt, but we *know* these resources are there, and we know that we can transform that country within ten years. And by transform I mean physically transform so people will not know it, in terms of health services, infrastructure, public services like functioning telephones.

BB-T: *That brings us to the question of corruption.*

WS: Yes, I was going to come to that. There's a philosophy of cannibalism in Nigeria at the moment, a ruthlessness towards each other. Market people – the moment there's a whisper there's going to be an increase in petrol price, even *before* it becomes a reality, they are already increasing the price of food. Even before the rumour is established! We are speaking here – the expression moral rearmament is so ugly because of its connotations with the past – but something is certainly required, call it ethical rearmament, call it human rearmament, we certainly need some kind of rearmament. And it can only begin with an improvement in the quality of life of people, with an evident commencement of transformation of the physical environment, and of course a reduction of corruption. Corruption has become even an *exhibitionist* fact. There is a level of exhibitionism in corruption which is unprecedented in Nigeria. Not even under Shagari – a totally corrupt government – has the level of corruption reached such heights. Not even in Shagari's era.

BB-T: *Where does Africa stand in what has been called the New World Order?*

WS: There will be no New World Order until the United Nations has been democratised. I believe very much that it's about time that the system is overhauled. The idea of giving some countries a permanent veto should go out with the New World Order. If the permanent veto is removed, it means that rationality can enter even the process of lobbying. In other words, issues will come more to the fore. Hopefully, the righteousness or the unrighteousness of issues will come more to the fore. Then the kind of muscle which is at present being displayed by permanent membership of the

Security Council will not have a place. A New World Order should also include a New Economic World Order. And this is where the issue of reparations becomes relevant. My position here tends to be rather ambiguous: I don't believe in aggressive beggary; I believe very passionately in the principle of paying one's debts. I just believe that the debts need to be examined very, very closely. If you are aiding a country to the tune of 1 million dollars, and three quarters of that million dollars goes towards servicing your own staff under the term 'expertise', then the word 'debt' should have a new definition. While I find the issue of reparations rather prob-lematic, there is a ring to it which ties up with a New World Order. When you create a New World Order, you're acknowledging certain impurities, certain flaws in the past relationship and you're saying, having acknowledged that, let us build a new relationship. If, for instance, we say the Old World Order was so tainted, we want to obliterate it and then we say we'll forget the past, *we* will annul the past, and *you* annul our so-called debts, and we'll call this the century of annulment and we move into the twenty-first century on a New World Order – which is not burdened by a deleterious economic past. We give ourselves, globally, a new chance. I believe in that kind of approach to a New World Order, not one that is dictated by the police actions of one superpower called the United States or China or whatever. It must also include a revitalisation of the de-colonisation process, because colonialism is not dead. You have even so-called Third World countries like Indonesia colonis-ing in East Timor and getting away with it. Brutalising the people there, committing massacres . . . When the United Nations is reformed that way, and there are no more double standards, then it will be possible to tackle issues like that and in effect even give ultimatums saying, look, if you want to participate in this New World Order which gives you an equal voice in the concert of nations, there are certain universal principles, such as a surrender of colonial possessions, which you must embrace and which you must execute, so it's not just the big powers alone I'm talking about. I'm talking about various pockets of re-colonisations, inhumanity. The incontestible universal areas – and there are many – of human rights have got to be acceded to. We cannot have this theory of relativity which some countries were trying to push at the last Vienna conference. You don't run tanks over sleeping students and come and tell me that human rights are relative. It's just impossible. And the same way Third World countries don't say, unless you help us we cannot develop, we cannot guarantee human rights. It's an obscene language. That's what I call the language of aggressive beggars.

BB-T: *The term 'ethnic cleansing' is one of this decade's contributions to language. Unfortunate as it is, it has been adopted sometimes unquestioningly even by liberal western press. There's all over Europe a resurgence of Fascism and Nazism. What are the implications for us all who are invariably the targets of these philosophies of hate?*

WS: I pity the European press their embarrassment. They find it difficult to accept that what happened in Nazi Germany is what is happening right now in certain parts of the world. Like Yugoslavia, for instance, and the former Soviet Union. And left to Saddam, I think he would have done some heavy 'ethnic cleansing' in northern Iraq by now. The whole world is a real mess, so many examples of 'ethnic cleansing' going on. It's a lesson for Europe and a lesson for us that these monsters are constantly with us and somehow have got to be exorcised. Both by state policies and by moral resolve among peoples. The resurgence of neo-Nazism does not surprise me in the slightest. It's always been lurking there. It exists in this country [UK], there are people in this country, even so-called intellectuals who would collaborate if there were to be some kind of fascist overturn in the government. Germany is the most naked, of course. Now Greece and Albania are at each other's throats, they're both performing their own form of 'ethnic cleansing'. And, let me use this chance to recall also that even in Nigeria, we have to a certain extent been guilty of a version of 'cleansing'. I refer to the Maroko episode, where three-quarters of a million people in Lagos were suddenly turned into non-people. Their dwellings, their entire habitation where they've lived for generations, were suddenly bulldozed in one fell swoop. I call that 'class sanitation'. It's another version of ethnic cleansing. It's a crime against humanity.

These various forms of de-humanisation are anomalies which have to be corrected before we can talk of any kind of New World Order.

BB-T: *Finally: who killed Dele Giwa?*[7]

WS: Who killed Dele Giwa? I'll tell you how Who Killed Dele Giwa will be exposed. It would be by the convening of the international jury which I've been working on. I've been taking advantage of my international contacts to try to set this up. In fact, we should have done it early this year but we had some problems. We have gathered the facts together. We will not say who killed Dele Giwa. We will leave the jury to decide whether the evidence we produce points definitely and unambiguously in one direction. If it fails, people will be able to decide whether or not the obvious suspects are guilty. It's no use naming anybody right now. Certain witnesses have fled the country. We know where they are, we know where some are, and they say they will come and give evidence when it's time. We intend to hold it in Nigeria; my present goal is on this year's anniversary of Dele Giwa's assassination. And the guilty parties know very well that all these enquiries have been taking place and are doing all they can to destroy evidence, but it's not going to help them. I resolved, when Dele Giwa was killed, that I would devote quite a large part of my time and resources to unearthing that crime, and it is my belief that we have done so.

1 Retired General Olusegun Obasanjo, Nigeria's Head-of-State 1976–79.

2 Leader of the Association for a Better Nigeria, which attempted to prevent the 12 June elections through the courts.

3 *Nigeria: Another Hope Betrayed.*

4 Henry Nwosu, Chairman, National Electoral Commission.

5 Alhaji Shehu Shagari, President, 1979–83.

6 Bisi Onabanjo, State Govenor during the last civilian government.

7 Editor of *Newswatch* magazine, murdered by a parcel bomb delivered at his house in October, 1986.

Excerpts from his interview appeared in *Index on Censorship*, volume 22, September–October, 1993.

Notes on Contributors

KWAME ANTHONY APPIAH was brought up in Ghana by Anglo-Ghanaian parents, and educated in England, where he took a double first in Philosophy at Cambridge University before writing his doctoral dissertation in the Philosophy of Language. He has taught at universities in Ghana and England, and now teaches at Harvard University. Professor Appiah is an editor of *Transition* and author of *Assertion and Conditionals*, *For Truth in Semantics*, *Necessary Questions* (an introduction to philosophy), *Avenging Angel* (a novel), and *In My Father's House: Africa in the Philosophy of Culture*. He is currently editing the *Oxford Book of African Literature*.

'BIYI BANDELE-THOMAS was born in Nigeria in 1967 and studied Drama at Obafemi Awolowo University, Ile Ife. He has published two novels, *The Man Who Came in from the Back of Beyond* and *The Sympathetic Undertaker and Other Dreams*, as well as several plays for both radio, television and the stage. He lives in London.

MARTIN BANHAM is Professor of Drama and Theatre Studies and the Director of the Workshop Theatre in the University of Leeds. He is also editor of *The Cambridge Guide to World Theatre*, and is presently writing a study of the theatre of Soyinka, Clark, Osofisan, Aidoo and Rotimi for the Cambridge University Press.

GABRIEL GBADAMOSI was born in 1961 in London of Irish/Nigerian parents, and studied Literature at Cambridge University. He now works as a poet and playwright. He lived in North Africa and took up a Winston Churchill Fellowship to travel across West Africa looking at theatre. He was awarded an Arts Council Arts Bursary in 1987, and was writer-in-residence at the Manchester Royal Exchange Theatre. Most recently he worked with the European Theatre Convention in Portugal, and is presently a Judith E. Wilson Fellow at Cambridge University. His plays include *No Blacks, No Irish*; *Shango*; *Abolition*; and *Eshu's Faust*, and a play for BBC television, *Friday's Daughter*. He has published poetry in various periodicals and anthologies, including *The New British Poetry*

1968–1988 (Paladin, 1988), and *The Heinemann Book of African Poetry in English* (William Heinemann, 1990).

NADINE GORDIMER was born and lives in South Africa. She has published ten novels and nine short story collections. She was awarded the Nobel Prize for Literature in 1991. She is a founder member and trustee of the Congress of South African Writers, a Vice-President of PEN International, and a member of the African National Congress.

ABDULRAZAK GURNAH was born in Zanzibar, Tanzania. He was educated there and in England and now teaches Literature at the University of Kent at Canterbury, England. He is the author of four novels: *Memory of Departure* (1987), *Pilgrims Way* (1988), and *Dottie* (1990). His latest novel, *Paradise*, was published in 1994 by Hamish Hamilton. He is also an Associate Editor of the journal *Wasafiri*.

WILSON HARRIS was born in New Amsterdam, British Guiana, in 1921. He qualified as a land surveyor and led many survey parties in the interior before he came to London in 1959. Faber & Faber have published his novels which include *Palace of the Peacock* (1960), *The Whole Armour* (1962), *Heartland* (1964), *The Waiting Room* (1967), *Ascent to Omai* (1970), *The Age of the Rainmakers* (1971), *The Tree of the Sun* (1978), *Carnival* (1985), *The Four Banks of the River of Space* (1990), and *Resurrection at Sorrow Hill* (1993). Other works include a collection of poems, *Eternity to Season* (1954), two collections of essays, *Tradition, the Writer and Society* (1967) and *Explorations* (1981), and a critical study, *The Womb of Space (The Cross-Cultural Imagination)* (1983). He has lectured at many universities in the UK, Australia and North America. He was awarded the CCH in 1991.

ADEWALE MAJA-PEARCE was born in London in 1953 and grew up in Lagos, Nigeria. His publications include *Loyalties and other stories* (1986), *In My Father's Country* (1987), *How Many Miles to Babylon?* (1990), *Who's Afraid of Wole Soyinka?* (1991), and *A Mask Dancing: Nigerian Novelists of the Eighties* (1992). He edited *Christopher Okigbo: Collected Poems* (1986), and *The Heinemann Book of African Poetry in English* (1990). He is editor of the Heinemann African Writers Series.

FEMI OSOFISAN *aka* Okinba Launko is a poet, novelist, playwright, actor, director and songwriter. He has also worked as a journalist, and runs a weekly Sunday column for one of Nigeria's national newspapers. Among his works are *The Chattering and the Song*, *Esu and the Vagabond Minstrels*, *Another Raft*, *Once Upon Four Robbers*, *Who's Afraid of Solarin?*, *Aringindin and the Nightwatchmen*, *Dreamseeker on Divining Chain*, *Cordelia* and the award-winning *Morountodun and Other Plays*, and *Minted Coins*. He is currently a Professor of Drama at the University of Ibadan, Nigeria.

NIYI OSUNDARE was born in Ikere-Ekiti, Nigeria, in 1947. He studied at universities in Nigeria, England and Canada, before taking up a post at the University of Ibadan in 1974, where he currently teaches. Between 1990 and 1992 he was a Fulbright Scholar at the University of New Orleans in the USA. He is a columnist for *Newswatch*, Nigeria's premier news magazine, and also for the *Sunday Tribune*. He has published eight volumes of poetry: *Songs of the Marketplace* (1983), *Village Voices* (1984), *A Nib in the Pond* (1986), *The Eye of the Earth* (1986; joint winner of the Commonwealth Poetry Prize), *Moonsongs* (1988), *Waiting Laughters* (1989; winner of the NOMA Award); *Selected Poems* (1992), and *Midlife* (1993).

Index